MACARTHUR: MAN OF ACTION

———————————————

STAR-SPANGLED MIKADO

MacArthur: MAN OF ACTION

FRANK KELLEY

CORNELIUS RYAN

DOUBLEDAY & COMPANY, INC., 1950

GARDEN CITY, NEW YORK

There is nothing in God's world
more sure than this:
Come what may, the United States
is not going to scuttle in the Pacific.

Contents

MACARTHUR: MAN OF ACTION

1. Come with Me . . .

It was raining that morning. Haneda airfield, just outside Tokyo, was a moist but chilly place even in the sticky early dawn. On the tarmac the C-54 with the word "Bataan" across its nose warmed up; a fine spray whipped up from the propellers, hung for a moment, then lashed back across the concrete runway. "The Old Man should be here any minute," a lieutenant shouted. Heads craned through windows for a glimpse; far off a convoy of vehicles churned through the early morning rain.

True, he was an "old man." He would be the last to deny it. At seventy age becomes a matter of reflection rather than denial. "Napoleon," he once said, "failed only because he was tired—the drive that kept him going was wearing out." Napoleon was only forty-six when he failed. But this general had never been given a chance to tire out; he had never given himself a chance to grow old in the strictly mental sense of the word.

On his desk is this framed message:

"Youth is not a time of life—it is a state of mind. Nobody grows old by merely living a number of years; people grow old only by deserting their ideals. Years wrinkle the skin, but to give no enthusiasm wrinkles the soul. Worry, doubt, self-distrust, fear, and despair—

these are the long, long years that bow the head and turn the growing spirit back to dust.

"Whether seventy or sixteen, there is in every being's heart the love of wonder, the sweet amazement at the stars and the starlike things and thoughts, the undaunted challenge of the events, the unfailing childlike appetite for what next, and the joy and the game of life.

"You are as young as your faith, as old as your doubt; as young as your self-confidence, as old as your fear; as young as your hope, as old as your despair."

And now on this rain-swept morning, this man of seventy, General of the Armies, Douglas MacArthur, Supreme Commander of the Allied Powers in Japan and United Nations Commander in Korea, was about to fly to the front where American troops with South Koreans, green and untried, were desperately trying to hold back a vicious, well-equipped enemy who ten days before had crossed the border from North to South Korea and thus placed the world on the edge of an abyss.

The convoy of cars pulled up by the plane. The General stepped out. He wore a leather jacket; his trousers had a knife-like edge. His hat, a famous hat embossed with heavy golden "scrambled eggs," seemed to lack sheen. His face was older, fuller; his eyes were hidden by sunglasses; his hands shook a little. But there was that same look of adventure, that same look of determination about the eyes that observers had seen before: Philippines, 1903; Mexico, 1914; the Western Front, 1918; Washington, 1930–35; Bataan, 1941; and all the blood-splashed islands of the Pacific of World War II. These were the eyes of the soldier. Turning to his aides and four correspondents, he said: "Gentlemen, we go."

Was this "we go" the "I shall return" of another war? Was this, in fact, really another war? Above them as they flew along four Mustangs, like eager terriers hunched together, flew wing tip to wing tip. Below them the choppy sea became a gray land raked hard by some giant who had forgotten to fill in the harsh fissures left behind. This was Korea—a land which five years before had been cut in half along a line of longitude as a military line of surrender; a line which cut the industrial head from the agricultural body of the country; a line which separated the ideology of the Kremlin from the Christianity of the West; a line which now meant death.

While the world slept in the uneasy slumber of a belief that mankind, despite his different ideologies, at heart had renounced war forever, tanks, troops, big guns, and all the paraphernalia of modern war swiftly moved across the 38th Parallel and brother was fighting against brother. The North Koreans were at war with the South Koreans. But there was far more to it than that: Korea had become Soviet Russia's vacuum cleaner, sucking the armed strength of the Western world, denuding areas where next they might incite a war. This was not going to be a clear-cut battle, but Americans would die —that was very clear.

The sound of the first shots in Korea had hardly died away before General MacArthur's critics began sniping from the side lines. One armchair strategist had this to say: "MacArthur was caught in the Philippine Islands despite . . . Pearl Harbor. And now, just as then, he has been caught flat-footed in Korea. . . . It appears the General did not even suspect that the Communists in North Korea were about to strike."

It would appear that the blame for the whole Korean war was MacArthur's for, added the writer, "Thanks to General MacArthur, South Korea was ill-prepared to defend herself." Others joined in that chorus, but the real truth seems to be that the whole world had been caught flat-footed.

A little checking on the part of MacArthur's critics would have shown that MacArthur has had no control over Korea for the past fifteen months, and Washington was warned that troops were massing on the 38th Parallel but the intelligence apparently failed to impress anybody of importance in the Pentagon. Either this must have happened, or the reports, which were routed from General MacArthur's headquarters, were never seen by those who could have made major decisions. For the Pentagon view before the attack was that the Korean peninsula would be all but impossible to hold against any sort of determined attack. Furthermore, it was felt that economically and politically it was not worth the effort. True, there was never any great enthusiasm in MacArthur's headquarters regarding Korea, but it is ridiculous to place the blame solely on him.

For two years MacArthur has warned of Communist preparedness in Asia. His words fell on deaf ears; so did his plea for more troops, arms, and air force units. But to his many critics it was MacArthur and he alone who was responsible for our lack of preparedness in the Far East. These critics would very much like an investigation held on his "stewardship," but they doubt if it will be held for the same reason that MacArthur was not investigated for the loss of the Philippines. He was not investigated, wrote one, "because American officials as well as American newspapers generally took the same view of MacArthur that he seems to have of himself:

that he is without peer; that he is a military and administrative genius such as never before has existed."

Controversy is nothing new in the life of General Douglas MacArthur. Today, at seventy, after the most consistently brilliant career of any American general of the last fifty years, instead of enjoying life in quiet retirement MacArthur is masterminding on the one hand the lives of 82,000,000 Japanese and with the other he is coolly running a war which holds great and terrifying portent for the whole world. Yet this general, on whom so much depends, is as controversial a figure today as he was the day he left West Point forty-seven years ago, when he graduated with the highest marks in twenty-five years of the Academy's history. He is probably the most beloved and most hated general on the entire American military stage.

The mere mention of his name—particularly in Washington—can incite either outbursts of superlatives pledging undying support, or bitter cries of vehement denunciation. There seems to be no happy middle ground, no in-between. With some—especially among his brother generals—the criticism sounds like jealousy; with others there is a deep-seated resentment born of rumor, legend, and fantasy. On the other side, there is absolute reverence and esteem.

There are those who claim that he is a "swash-buckling, overdressed, egotistical, outdated Alexander the Great who thinks he has deistic qualities," and others who describe him as a "modern Julius Caesar radiating glamour like a Barrymore in khaki . . . no coarse, tobacco-stained, whisky-guzzling Ulysses Grant . . . here is a magnificent leader with unrivaled political perception, unequaled military skill." Perhaps he is part of both schools of thought.

Like all leaders, especially those who suddenly find themselves caught squarely in the spotlight of world attention time and time again, MacArthur will always be subject to adulation and hatred. His every action, word, and communiqué increases the fury of the ever-boiling cauldron of controversy. Yet one thing stands clear: few have ever belittled his military achievements. General George C. Marshall thought of him as "our most brilliant general." The late James Forrestal saw in him "America's beachhead in Asia—our greatest strategist." Churchill called him "a glorious commander." Few generals have done so much with so little, and that is recognized by his most hardened critics. It is not, therefore, his military prowess or generalship which sparks the controversy; it is caused by a number of factors, some of them quite intangible, which make up the General's character.

Some observers have tried to draw comparisons between the late President Roosevelt and General MacArthur. They claim that history will paint Roosevelt as a great statesman and a bad president; MacArthur a great general and a bad politician. Perhaps this is so. Both men are legendary, but F.D.R.'s saga is more definite. Roosevelt endeared himself to the great mass of the American public because of his vibrant, warm personality; they felt close to him, part of him, and he was approachable. Not so General MacArthur. Knowingly or unknowingly, MacArthur gives the impression of being a man on a mountaintop shrouded in clouds of drama, so far above his fellow man as to appear quite unapproachable. It is this impression of cold dramatic aloofness, more than anything else, which makes him the subject of so much controversy.

The American public knows MacArthur only in times

of crisis. He is a last-stand general, an into-the-breach general who is called upon to perform fantastic miracles with the absolute minimum of men and equipment. He must never make a mistake, for mistakes are not expected of him; he must be farsighted and shrewd; he must be statesman as well as general. MacArthur has created this character both in Washington and in the public mind; he must live with it.

As a result of this his every act becomes a *cause célèbre*. What would pass unnoticed in another general's theater of operations becomes a headline in Mac-Arthur's. Thus his every move appears charged with dramatic intensity. True, MacArthur has an excellent sense of timing and knows when to pull back the velvet curtains and step dramatically into the spotlight. But much of the theater-charged atmosphere which surrounds him is exaggerated to a great extent by well-meaning but often ill-advised staff officers.

General MacArthur is a stern commander who demands and receives unswerving loyalty. It has been charged, therefore, that MacArthur likes only "yes" men around him; that those who disagree too violently are cast into exterior darkness. Certainly during World War II certain minor staff officers acted in such idolatrous ways and spoke of the "Old Man" in such honey-dripping terms as to give support to the "yes men" theory. However, this could not be said for men of the caliber of General Krueger, General Eichelberger, General Thorpe, General Dyke, to mention just a few. Neither does it hold good today for men such as Lieutenant General Walton H. Walker, a lusty, colorful tank expert who led General Patton's 20th Corps across the battlefields of Europe; nor for General George E. Stratemeyer, commander of the Far East Air Force,

who, like his predecessor, Lieutenant General George
C. Kenney, is a man with the courage of his own con-
victions.

Yet bad staff work by one officer, whose name Mac-
Arthur has never revealed, resulted in harsh criticism
and added yet another chapter to the MacArthur legend.
This centered on the famous Leyte speech made when
the General stepped onto the invasion beach. Those
who were with him say that his voice shook with genuine emotion as he spoke into the microphone.

"This is the Voice of Freedom, General MacArthur
speaking . . . I have returned. By the grace of Almighty
God our forces stand again on Philippine soil. The
hour of your redemption is at hand. Rally to me! As
the lines of battle roll forward to bring you within the
zones of operation, rise and strike! For your homes and
hearths, strike! For future generations of your sons and
daughters, strike! In the name of your sacred dead,
strike! Let no heart be faint. Let every arm be steeled.
The guidance of Divine God points the way. Follow in
His name to the Holy Grail of righteous victory."

This speech was never intended for United States
consumption. It was aimed directly at the Filipinos.
Yet because of the inefficiency of the undisclosed staff
officer who probably thought that every word pearl
dropped from the General's lips should be immediately
disseminated, the speech reached the outside world.

We can believe that MacArthur had no thought in
mind other than to rally the Filipinos. He knows the
people better than any other military officer; he knows
the psychology of the Filipinos probably better than
any other living American. The hero worshiping of his
father, General Arthur MacArthur, had been transferred to him from the moment he set foot in the

islands three months after getting his commission as a second lieutenant. The Filipinos, a deeply religious people, had last heard MacArthur's voice three years before from the Voice of Freedom station deep in a tunnel on the rocky fastness of Corregidor. That message had been as dramatic as the Leyte speech: "We shall rise in the name of freedom and the East shall be alight with the glory of our liberation." They remembered, too, his world-famous "I shall return" speech made when he landed in Australia. Psychological warfare experts today say that the Leyte speech was precisely the right kind of spirit-lifting and morale-building call to action that the Filipinos needed. It was worth perhaps an extra division of men. With his expert showmanship and richly modulated voice—deep one moment, rising in crescendo the next—he knew best how to lend emphasis to his instructions to the Filipino people, but he was criticized here for too flamboyant prose.

Those who have met MacArthur and talked with him will agree that, despite his love for the dramatic, he would not have approved, either officially or unofficially, the release to the world of the Leyte speech.

Compare, for example, the straightforward simplicity of his address made after the signing of the articles of surrender on board the battleship *Missouri.* "It is my earnest hope, and indeed the hope of mankind," said General MacArthur, "that from this solemn occasion a better world shall emerge out of the blood and carnage of the past—a world founded on faith and understanding—a world dedicated to the dignity of man and the fulfillment of his most cherished wish for freedom, tolerance, and justice."

The Leyte speech was jumped on by MacArthur critics. It was denounced as "sacrilegious and uncalled for" by the more charitable; others made it more personal, promptly dubbed him "God's Cousin." But MacArthur stood by the officer who had allowed the speech radio clearance.

Again and again MacArthur was criticized for his public statements in which he insistently invoked the name of the Deity. This, plus his majestic aloofness, gave rise to the famous Marine poem which ended with the verse:

> And while possibly a rumor now,
>   Someday it will be fact
> That the Lord will hear a deep voice say,
>   Move over God, it's Mac.

The Navy, too, laid emphasis on the General's "Bible-pounding." In a parody on the "Battle Hymn of the Republic" one wit wrote these lines:

> Mine eyes have seen MacArthur
>   With a Bible on his knee,
> A-typin' out communiqués
>   For guys like you and me.
> "Our heavy bombers hit Rabaul
>   And God is filled with glee!"
> While Mac goes marching on.

In every other theater of war there were poems of similar character, but nobody paid any attention to them, least of all the staff officers. If the headquarters of Generals Eisenhower, Bradley, Patton, Montgomery, *et al.* had worried about foxhole parodies they would have had little time to conduct a war. MacArthur, if he knew of the jibes, cared little and probably would have taken them for what they were intended: good-natured kidding. But many junior staff officers let it be quietly known that the "Old Man" highly disapproved, thus increasing the importance and popularity of the stories and furthering another choice segment to the legend.

The Air Force is charged with being responsible for the term "Dugout Doug." This was a belittling of Mac-Arthur's courage, completely unjustified and uncalled for. MacArthur can be criticized for many faults, but certainly not on the subject of his personal bravery. He has never been known to wear a helmet, even in World War I. In that bloody conflict he was called the "most daring brigade commander on the Western Front," and won the D.S.C. twice for bravery in action. Like his father before him, MacArthur holds the nation's highest military distinction—the Congressional Medal of Honor.

There was, however, great justification in the navy and air force charges that MacArthur's communiqués described them as "my navy" and "my air force." This caused intense bitterness among all ranks, including senior officers, of both proud services. The Marines, too, had their complaints. They felt that they had been completely forgotten, called themselves "MacArthur's guinea pigs."

The Navy particularly disliked the General. The former Secretary of War, Henry L. Stimson (1940–45), writing in his book *On Active Service in Peace and War* on navy disagreements said that "MacArthur was a constant bone of contention. . . . The extraordinary brilliance of the officer was not always matched by his tact, but the Navy's astonishing bitterness toward him seemed childish."

Always conscious of his place in history and abnormally sensitive to press criticism of any kind,[1] Mac-

[1] As evidenced in his 1934 libel suit against columnists Pearson and Allen, wherein MacArthur asked for $1,750,000 on seven charges, varying from the assertion that he had "proposed to

Arthur or his press officers—it is extremely difficult to draw a dividing line—made one blunder after another. Correspondents were made to observe the strictest censorship imposed in any theater of operations throughout the war world. Perhaps mindful of World War II censorship, MacArthur issued an announcement at the start of the Korean war asserting that censorship was "abhorrent" and proposed a "voluntary code" for the correspondents which called for them to avoid the mentioning of troop movements and locations of headquarters among other things. Within a few weeks, however, correspondents were asking for a security censorship, for, as Lindesay Parrott of the New York *Times* wrote, "the question is whether under wartime conditions the peacetime privileges of the free press can be permitted to prevail in the face of the dangers to soldiers' lives that irresponsibility of even honestly mistaken reporting can produce."

In World War II, however, a stringent censorship was undoubtedly necessary, for MacArthur's command covered an area twenty-five times larger than the state of Texas, but the censorship was such that nothing of a derogatory nature could be said about MacArthur. When censorship was finally lifted—six months after the ending of Pacific hostilities—the ensuing blast from long pent-up correspondents who, at one time or another, had been called "two-bit sports writers" among other things, blew MacArthur's chief press officer off his perch. This seemed to give truth to the feeling that

---

some of his congressional friends a new law requiring 19-gun salutes for former chiefs of staff" to the charge that he "chafed because he wasn't being promoted fast enough." There was no trial, and the suit was dropped after Pearson and Allen reported that no money was paid to MacArthur for costs or otherwise, no apologies or retractions given or asked for.

MacArthur, too, was learning the actual state of his public-relations department for the first time. Many felt that had MacArthur's press officers but realized that the General's greatness needed little embellishment, the over-all effect would have been much better. Furthermore, his marked sense of showmanship—whether natural or by design—plus the fact that he was tossed into dramatic situations, such as Bataan, through no fault of his own, automatically made good headline copy. His military achievements simply spoke for themselves, yet his public-relations officers insisted on gilding the lily. MacArthur needed no gilding.

His personal appearance, his physique, and dignified bearing have even been criticized. In Australia he was accused of being overdressed, because he wore full-dress uniform with eleven rows of medals. Nobody criticized Eisenhower, Patton, or Montgomery for wearing full dress. The General has not worn full dress since. Today he invariably wears suntans, the only embellishment the famous "scrambled-egg" cap which he is said to have designed. This, too, has had its share of criticism, yet it is interesting to note that the new uniform of the Air Force calls for senior officers to wear caps very much like the MacArthur variety.

MacArthur's personal life, too, has had its share of comment. Few people from the outside have ever grown close to him. Correspondents in Tokyo see him rarely and only by appointment made weeks and sometimes months in advance. He is not an accessible man. Once in his presence, however, he simply magnetizes. He strides up and down the floor of his office on the sixth floor of the Dai Ichi Building, knuckling his thinning hair as he talks. He will strike perhaps six matches before pausing long enough to light the ever-present corncob pipe. His hands are thin and finely wrinkled now, but they sweep through the air with vigor and forcefulness as he gesticulates to make a point. He will talk on any subject brilliantly, and what begins as a five-minute interview can stretch to half an hour or an hour. It is generally a very one-sided conversation. You do not talk *with* MacArthur; he talks *at* you.

He does not joke easily. He can see the humor in a situation or series of events, but he will barely smile when told a story with an amusing ending. He can be a very warm and human person in a private interview, so much so that often the visitor wonders where he first got the impression that MacArthur was aloof. But the moment the interview is over he becomes the "man on the mountaintop" again. Those who meet him for the first time leave his office completely hypnotized, muttering words such as "genius," "brilliant," "great." For here is MacArthur's real forte.

Some of his most hardened critics have come out from his office completely converted. By his very brilliance in conversation one truly gets the impression of being in the presence of greatness. Perhaps this feeling arises because MacArthur *acts out* every part. At one moment he is bitter and his voice shakes with denunciation; the next moment it is soft and sentimental; then deep and resonant as he pontificates. Always the great moment, the one that is remembered, comes when he talks of the United States and its place in Asia, particularly as far as Japan is concerned. His voice takes on a ringing note as he paints a picture of Japan being Asia's "bulwark" for America. He is convinced that he is building a model democracy in Japan which will be so perfect that it will point the way toward world peace. Japan "is the springboard of the future . . . our frontier lies here in Asia where more than half the world's population lives . . . we haven't begun to realize its vast potentialities."

Some have criticized his methods in Japan, claiming that you can't hold a hand up one day to a people who have been running 2,000 years in one direction and say "stop! Go this way!" MacArthur thinks it can be done, and in the last five years he has gone a long way toward proving it. Few, indeed, could have done a better job.

There are millions throughout the world who think of MacArthur as an "egotistical dictator," but, with the exception of the "old-school kimono boys," he is worshiped by the Japanese. They tell him so, too, in thousands of letters, on every subject imaginable, which arrive at his headquarters each week. Yet MacArthur has never toured the country. With the exception of a trip in 1948 to Korea and his dramatic flights to the front recently, MacArthur has been at his desk in Tokyo seven days a week, ten hours a day, for the last five years.

Few people realize that he has not set foot in his homeland since 1937. The nearest he has been to the United States was during the war, when he conferred with President Roosevelt at Hawaii. Furthermore, MacArthur has not had a complete vacation since the beginning of the Pacific struggle. Many another man would have long since cracked under the strain. The uncharitable rarely remember these things.

Perhaps the one event which still rankles MacArthur is his flight from Bataan to Australia in a PT-boat. Ordered out by presidential order, his famous dash across the Pacific resulted in harsh and unjust criticism from many quarters. Judging from many of the stories that were written on the amount of worldly goods the

MacArthurs took with them one would think that they surely must have used a freighter. Just for the record: besides MacArthur, wife, child, and Chinese nurse, they took one mattress (because Mrs. MacArthur was ill) and four suitcases. That story, too, has become part of the controversy.

MacArthur has rarely answered his detractors. Thus much of the fact and legend which surround him must remain for proper evaluation by future historians and biographers. He once said: "You are only remembered and become famous because of your mistakes." MacArthur will be remembered for more than his mistakes. Meanwhile, until the definitive history of MacArthur is painted, his critics might do worse than to study what has been called "MacArthur's Credo"—a framed piece by the Roman historian Livy which hangs in the Supreme Commander's office. Here is the true character of MacArthur today. The piece tells how a famous Roman general who had been ordered to conduct a war in Macedonia in 168 B.C. told off his critics. Directly after he had been appointed by the Roman senate, after much denunciation and criticism (apparently senate investigations were not unknown even then), he marched out into the rotunda, where his detractors had gathered, and said:

"Commanders should be counseled chiefly by persons of known talent; by those who have made the art of war their particular study, and whose knowledge is derived from experience; by those who are present at the scene of action, who see the enemy, who see the advantages that occasions offer, and who like people embarked on the same ship are sharers of the danger. If, therefore, anyone thinks himself qualified to give advice respecting the war which I am to conduct, let him not refuse assistance to the state . . . but come with me to Macedonia.

"He shall be furnished with a ship, a horse, a tent; even his traveling charges shall be defrayed. But if he thinks this too much trouble and prefers the repose of the city life to the toils of war, let him not on land assume the office of pilot.

"The city in itself furnishes abundance of topics for conversation; let it confine its passion for talking to its own precincts and rest assured that we shall pay no attention to any counsel but such as shall be framed within our camp."

2. Father MacArthur

The MacArthurs spring from a long line of warriors who can trace themselves back to Robert the Bruce. In fact there is an old Scottish proverb which says, "Nothing has stood longer than MacArthur, the hills, and the devil." But the more up-to-date military history of the MacArthurs begins with Douglas MacArthur's father, the late Lieutenant General Arthur MacArthur—boy hero of our Civil War, conqueror of Aguinaldo in the Philippines at the turn of the century, and recipient, in 1901, of the surrendered sword of another Filipino insurrectionist, Manuel Quezon. Thirty-five years later the same Quezon, then President of the Philippines, handed to Douglas MacArthur the gold baton of a field marshal of the Philippine Army.

Arthur MacArthur, the only son of Scottish-born Judge Arthur MacArthur, was born at Springfield, Massachusetts, on June 2, 1845. He was taken to Wisconsin in 1849 by his father, who practiced law there, became lieutenant governor of Wisconsin and later judge of the District of Columbia Supreme Court.

In 1861 the Civil War broke out. Arthur was not yet sixteen, but was determined to get into it. His father hired a detective to see that the lad did not run away. But in August 1862, when the boy was seventeen, the father consented and got him a commission as first lieutenant and adjutant of the 24th Wisconsin Volunteer Infantry.

An old affectionate account, written some years later, says the boy was a stripling in size and with a stripling's effeminate voice and manners . . . to make a long story short, the little adjutant became a laughing-stock solely on account of what nature hadn't done for him up to that time.

"One bit of camp gossip had it that the colonel said one day, in a fit of disgust, that he'd ask Governor Salo-mon to send him a wooden man or any old thing for adjutant and take the boy back to Milwaukee and put him in an army kindergarten. If the colonel did say that, it was the best thing that he ever did for the regi-ment. We were in quiet camp at Louisville then and hadn't struck the fighting. Well, the boy heard what the colonel said, or was alleged to have said, and there were no more mincing or falsetto commands on parade drill. Arthur changed to a man in a night, and I can imagine how it was with him, for I was only a kid my-self then. . . .

"Well, in the case of Arthur, it didn't take long to prove the truth of Davy Crockett's saying about battle-field courage. 'Pluck,' said the border hero, 'doesn't de-pend on the length of one's beard, otherwise a goat would be a better fighter than any man.'

"We got into our first good fight at Stone's River, with Sheridan's division. Somehow I have forgotten the de-tails of it. Our Colonel and Lieutenant Colonel were not on hand, and the regiment was handled that day by Major Hibbard and the boy adjutant, Arthur Mac-Arthur. It was fight and retreat, then rally and make a stand until flanked, then retreat again, rally again and fight again, from daylight until dark.

"Finally, when the ammunition was all used and the ranks down to fragments, Little Phil ordered what there was left of the division back to the railroad entrenchments. Our remnant looked like the parts of a sail which a gale of wind leaves clinging to the spars when it strips a vessel of its canvas, just a fringe of men on each side of the flagstaff.

"But say! that boy Arthur was in his element and proved to be anything else but a kindergartener. The regiment lost fully half of the four hundred and odd men carried into battle, and that day's work made the beardless adjutant a hero in the eyes of the whole brigade.

"Our commandant, Major Hibbard, devoted a paragraph of his official report to the praise of little Arthur MacArthur. Said he: 'To the adjutant of the regiment I am more than indebted for his aid and efficient service rendered during the engagements. I bespeak for him an honorable career.'

"Stone's River was an unequal fight for our division. The trouble began when it was discovered about daylight that the enemy had surprised our right flank and turned it and was in our rear. In the first column of attack, which our regiment received alone, we counted five Confederate battle flags. Seven times that day we formed line of battle under fire. Our brigade commander, General Joshua Sill, was killed at the outset, and at one time we took orders from Sheridan direct. Colonel Nick Greusel, the sturdy Illinois fighter, assumed command soon after General Sill was killed, and in his official report told how Adjutant Arthur MacArthur Jr., of the 24th Wisconsin, displayed 'great coolness and presence of mind' in that terrible day of battle. So the regiment came out of it with a record equal to that of the best of Sheridan's seasoned troops, and we were glad indeed that our boy adjutant hadn't been traded off for a wooden man before we left Louisville."

In the northern attack at Missionary Ridge, MacArthur was in the thickest of the fray. This was Sheridan's great fight in the west, and the Milwaukee boys were in the heat of the charge that carried the line up the height.

"It was a sort of San Juan Hill impulse which moved our whole division up," the old account continues, "for the orders were simply to capture the enemy's works at the base of the hill and then halt. Well, that order was carried out literally. The men rested for breath a bit and then was heard the cry, 'We can't live here! We must go forward!' and forward we went.

"Wagner's brigade, on the left of us, was actually turned back midway of the ridge by a staff officer carrying out the instructions to the letter. But Sheridan saw that we on the right were in for it and sent Wagner forward again. Just before that Sheridan had told a staff officer from headquarters who came to inquire by what authority the troops were charging the main heights: 'I didn't order them up, but we are going to take this ridge.'

"It was hot work, and no mistake. The ground was broken and rough and we couldn't keep a line, so we clung together in groups, all the time moving uphill under fire. As someone said of the San Juan Hill fight it was a climb, not a charge. But men went down fast enough for the hottest charge, among them our colorbearer. We were near the crest, and it happened that at the moment there was confusion in the minds of some as to the best way to go to strike the enemy's works. Roads and ravines being the least obstructed invited us there, but they were swept by the enemy's sharpest fire. By that time, too, the men were winded and they stopped and looked back. We really had no line; the charge has been compared to the flight of migratory birds. We saw that we had done an unusual thing, breaking ranks and running forward helter-skelter.

"When our flag went down there was nothing whatever to rally our line upon, and then the boy adjutant made the second hit of his career in the Twenty-fourth. He seized the staff and waved the flag for a moment as a signal to rally on the center, then darted forward to the very crest and into a battery, the leader of the whole line, the foremost of sixty battle flags then moving up the slope.

"As we neared the summit we were under the muzzles of the big guns at General Bragg's headquarters, but the slope was so steep that the pieces could not be depressed sufficiently to harm us. However, the Johnnies bowled lighted shells down upon our heads. But we held the ridge, and to Sheridan's division were awarded those guns as battle trophies.

"As for Arthur MacArthur, there is a record in the War Department which says: 'Medal of Honor to Arthur MacArthur for coolness and conspicuous bravery in action in seizing the colors of his regiment at a critical moment and planting them on the captured works on the crest of Missionary Ridge, Tennessee, November 25, 1863, while serving as first lieutenant and adjutant, Twenty-fourth Wisconsin Infantry.' "

There would have been trouble in the regiment, wrote the old-timer, if any new deal in field officers left out Arthur MacArthur after that exploit. He was promoted to major before the next hot fight at Kenesaw and commanded the regiment that day and afterward until a bullet laid him low on November 30, 1864. He would have been killed had not a packet of letters in his breast pocket stopped the bullet. There was a legend among survivors of the 24th that MacArthur's commission as major was in the packet of letters and that the bullet left its black mark right over the name where the document read: "To Arthur MacArthur, greeting."

Arthur MacArthur led his regiment in another hot fight at Franklin, Tennessee. He swung into his saddle, sabering the gray-clad Confederates right and left to cut a path to the front. When the smoke cleared, he was found lying helpless, wounded.

They couldn't commission MacArthur a full colonel, because the regiment could not muster enough men. But they gave him the brevet rank with the commission of lieutenant colonel, and it was he who took the regiment home to Milwaukee in 1865.

MacArthur immediately entered the regular army as a second lieutenant and fought the Indians for twenty years.

His son Douglas was born January 26, 1880, on the father's post at Little Rock barracks, Arkansas. He was only four when his mother and a company sergeant protected him from bows and arrows of Indians raiding his father's army barracks in New Mexico. And with the breakfast oatmeal and milk young Douglas sopped up much of the history of the Civil War along with lectures on tactics.

Late in the century Arthur MacArthur—then a lieutenant colonel and an adjutant general—realized that a war with Spain was impending. He promptly made his plans to get to the front. On April 24, 1898, when

Congress declared war against Spain, MacArthur was recommended for the commission of brigadier general by the entire Wisconsin delegation. The delegation also called upon President McKinley at the White House and asked for two appointments of brigadier general of volunteers. One was for MacArthur; the other for a retired captain, Charles King, an author. Both were commissioned and sent to the Philippines.

With one blow General Arthur MacArthur captured the town and bridges of Malate, thereby forming the opening wedge for the taking of Manila. (In 1945 his son, Douglas, sent the 1st Cavalry Division—now in action in Korea—on an end run into Manila from the north to liberate 4,000 Americans and other nationals from the Santo Tomas internment camp and to lead the way for retaking the city from the Japanese.)

"It was no such fighting as we had in 1863–64," MacArthur wrote. But he applied the tactics he had learned after many a hard scout seeking Comanche and Apache through New Mexican and Arizona wilds. He was advanced to major general almost from the day of his arrival in Manila. In March 1900 he was assigned to command all the American forces in the islands and at the same time was named military governor.

Almost immediately he set about the task of laying the foundation for rehabilitation of the Philippine people. He began to install a system of education, law, and justice for the islanders. He helped to give them that priceless feature of Anglo-Saxon jurisprudence: the writ of habeas corpus. He started a native defense force, the Philippine Scouts.

In 1901 President McKinley sent William Howard Taft, then a Federal Circuit Court judge, later President of the United States, out to the Philippines as governor general. He, too, did a lot to pacify the Filipinos, to improve their economic lot, and to start them toward self-government.

Taft and Arthur MacArthur did not get along. One was the civil boss, the other was military commander. Their clashes were many and animated. MacArthur was relieved in July 1901 and returned home. In due course Taft returned, too, and became Secretary of War in 1904.

By 1906 Arthur MacArthur was a lieutenant general, the highest grade he achieved. He had commanded successively the Department of Lakes, the Department of the East, the Department of California (where he had to welcome Taft home from Manila via San Francisco), and then the newly created Division of the Pacific. When he was relieved of that in 1907 (Taft was still running the War Department) General MacArthur was without an adequate command. He should have become Chief of Staff in Washington. Taft preferred General J. F. Bell. MacArthur, realizing he was destined to duty not in accord with his rank, obtained a nominal assignment to prepare a report, with permission to reside in Milwaukee.

On June 2, 1909, Lieutenant General Arthur MacArthur retired at the age of sixty-four. William Howard Taft had by then passed a few months in the White House as the hand-picked successor of Theodore Roosevelt.

The New York *Evening Post* bade farewell to General MacArthur, with this sub-headline: "The Lieutenant General Who Goes Out an Accomplished Gentleman, an Admirable Officer, and a Splendid General."

His death in Milwaukee on September 6, 1912, was as dramatic as his life had been upon the battlefield. Despite his physician's orders, General MacArthur attended the fiftieth annual reunion of his old Civil War regiment. Called upon to speak at the banquet, he said he would give his last tribute to his old comrades. He recalled the deeds of the 24th Wisconsin Infantry in the Atlanta campaign.

"Your indomitable courage . . ." He paused a few seconds. "Comrades, I am too weak to go on." He sank back into his chair and died in a few seconds of an apoplectic stroke. The hundred-odd old soldiers stood in shocked silence for a moment. Then they rushed to the General's side. They found his eyes closed, his lips silent.

MacArthur's old adjutant, Captain Edwin B. Parsons, who had been standing at his side, collapsed with a paralytic stroke at the shock of seeing the General fall. He was carried out.

With tear-filled eyes the others knelt at MacArthur's side and murmured the Lord's Prayer. One of them took down the Stars and Stripes from the wall and spread it over the dead commander.

3. The Women Behind MacArthur

Two well-dressed, dignified ladies met in the hall of Craney's Hotel at West Point. They greeted each other effusively—too effusively. There was just the slightest note of wary respect in their pleasantries. They swept out of the hotel together and went their separate ways. Both glanced back, appraising the other's gown, then, caught in the act, smiled in embarrassment. Mrs. Ulysses S. Grant II and Mrs. Arthur MacArthur, proud bearers of two of the greatest names in American military history, were fighting one of the most lady-like but most bitter campaigns West Point had ever seen.

It was the year 1899. Ulysses S. Grant III and young Douglas MacArthur were competing for top honors of their class. It was the first year at West Point for both, and their respective mothers were proving far more tenacious in their demands than any instructor at the Point. Much was expected from both youths, and their mothers were on hand to see that the great expectations materialized.

There was another aspect to the fierce competitive spirit of the two ladies. Mary Pinkney Hardy MacArthur came from the South, though she had "crossed the border" when she married the dashing young soldier, Captain Arthur MacArthur, twenty-four years before.

At heart she was still a proud Southerner, and the name Grant did not set too well with her. It would be such a triumph if her son "Dougie," as she called him, won the scholastic battle. Mrs. Ulysses S. Grant II was "conscious" of Mrs. MacArthur and of the fact that General Arthur MacArthur "had made quite a name for himself" in the Philippines, where, incidentally, he was at this period, but it appears that Mrs. Grant would have liked to believe that the MacArthurs were not quite members of the Army's 400. Yet she and Mrs. Mac-Arthur were "devoted" to each other.

It is doubtful whether the two boys were aware of the velvet-glove campaign waged for their benefit (though the cadet corps used to say: "They're hair pullin' again"). They were good friends, studied hard, and lived the rigid life expected of them. But they were both conscious of their proud family heritage; they were both out to win top honors. Young Grant, however, never quite topped MacArthur. That first year MacArthur was head of his class and Grant was second. That was the nearest Grant ever came. MacArthur swept the board of all honors; in their final year Grant came in only seventh.

While this was a triumph for MacArthur, it was fully *expected* by his mother. For whatever else appears about Mary Pinkney Hardy MacArthur, one thing is clear: she was sweet, meek, and pretty, but she had a remarkable habit of getting what she went after. There seems to have been no doubt in her mind that her son was going to come out on top.

Whatever the character of MacArthur, the molder of much of it was his mother. From his father he seems to have inherited courage, stamina, and a love of books; from his mother he acquired not only brilliance and determination, but also a shyness which few people are aware that he possesses.

Mary Pinkney Hardy came from a very aristocratic Virginia family steeped in the traditions of the old South. Stanch supporters of the Confederacy, all the male Hardys fought under Lee. Thus it was something of a shock when she fell in love with a young soldier from the North, dashing young Captain Arthur MacArthur. That the family tried to dissuade her from the marriage seems obvious, for on the day of the wedding, May 19, 1875, her brothers, still loyal to their southern heritage, refused to attend the ceremony. If this hurt the young bride of twenty-two she never revealed it—she had decided on Arthur MacArthur and she married him. That was the way of Mary Pinkney Hardy.

Douglas was born five years after the marriage. "My first recollection," he is fond of telling, "is that of a bugle call." Everything around him had to do with a military way of life. Indeed, as mentioned elsewhere in this book, the first time he ever experienced an attack from an enemy came when he was only four years old. During an Indian raid on a fort in New Mexico an arrow came perilously close to him. His mother ran with him in her arms as the first shower of feathered missiles came whistling into the compound. But Douglas, according to various accounts, enjoyed every minute of the raid.

His first books had to do with soldiering; his playmates were the children of other soldiers on the post, and, like young Douglas, their first playground was an army square. Soldiering was born in MacArthur, and the love and determination of his mother brought it to full flower within him.

There were two other boys in the family; one died when a child; the other, Arthur MacArthur III, became a lieutenant commander in the Navy. He died in 1923. Douglas became the only son and was much favored. There was an intenseness about him from the very start. He was absolutely devoted to his mother and she, in turn, to him. They were inseparable; up to the day she died, at the age of eighty-two, in 1935, she was undoubtedly the most powerful influence in MacArthur's life. Indeed all who knew her say that but for her brilliant management of the boy when he was in his teens MacArthur would not be the military statesman he is today.

There was something of the Scarlett O'Hara in Mary MacArthur. She was petite, charming, and tough. She could be petulant, sentimental, and emotional all at the same time, yet always remain cool and practical beneath. She passed these traits on in one complex bundle to Douglas MacArthur.

No estimate of MacArthur's character can be made by any future biographer unless a complete study is made of Mary MacArthur. For with her lay the seed of leadership which was firmly implanted in her son. With her, too, was the pride of family which MacArthur was never allowed to forget for one minute. He was told again and again that his father was one of America's greatest soldiers; that he was going to exceed even his father's record. That the youth was awed by what was expected of him there can be little doubt. Some of the family's closest friends, without any intention of being derogatory, have expressed the opinion that the egoism so often criticized in MacArthur's make-up is nothing more than a barrier which he has erected to hide his own natural shyness. They carry this theory further and point out that it explains why he has been so extremely sensitive to criticism in the past. All this they attribute to the remarkable influence of his mother, maintaining that in the furtherance of his career she had no time for weakness or natural bent which the boy might have had.

It so happened that his natural bent was for a military life. This, plus a truly remarkable brain and the driving power and emotional qualities of his mother, produced Douglas MacArthur.

Mary MacArthur tutored her son as a child to make West Point and the Army his goal. His years of study, first at Texas Military Academy, later at West Point, were entirely supervised by Mrs. MacArthur. No obstacle was insurmountable to her. When young Douglas failed to pass the West Point medical examination because of a spinal defect and was rejected by the Academy, his mother promptly took him to the best doctors in Milwaukee—nominally the family seat—and had him treated until he was fully recovered. During this period his studies were not neglected. Part of the time he went to West Division High School and the remainder of his pre-West Point coaching was done by Mary MacArthur. The following year he entered the Academy.

There, too, his mother supervised his studies. Indeed he spent most of his off hours with her, but not all of them. Somehow during the three years he found time to become engaged to eight girls all at the same time. Once, when asked about it, he wryly admitted: "I have never been so hotly engaged by the enemy." While Mary MacArthur's family had been unsuccessful in preventing her marriage to Arthur MacArthur, her vigilance over Douglas's early romances apparently saved him from the wrath of eight unnamed young ladies and their families.

MacArthur did not become officially engaged until

1922. Oddly enough he was back at West Point, this time as the Academy's youngest superintendent. He was then, at forty, a brigadier general, having won his spurs on the battlefields of Europe, and the youngest superintendent in West Point's history. His mother was not with him when he met Mrs. Walter Brooks, Jr., of Baltimore, the former Louise Cromwell, who had just obtained a Paris divorce.

Mrs. Louise Cromwell Brooks had been born to society and had attended costly finishing schools. She was a stepdaughter of E. T. Stotesbury, the Philadelphia multimillionaire. Her coming-out party was one of the most elaborate in society and was one of the most talked-about events in Washington. The restaurant where it was held—Rauscher's at Connecticut and L Street—was converted into a garden with cedar trees, asparagus ferns, palms, and roses; and to top the whole thing off—live yellow canaries.

Her marriage to Walter Brooks, Jr., had lasted eight years, during which they had two children. In 1919 she left for France, where she got a divorce. There in the company of her brother, James Cromwell (later to be the husband of Doris Duke and United States Minister to Canada), she mixed with the international set and met, among other people, General "Black Jack" Pershing, who found her attractive and entertaining. When she returned to America she became Pershing's official hostess in Washington, and for a time society circles thought that the twenty-five-year-old divorcée and the sixty-year-old general would announce their engagement. Then she met General MacArthur. He proposed to her the first night he met her.

Years later the former Mrs. Douglas MacArthur had this to say about the General's proposal: "If he hadn't proposed the first time we met, I believe I would have done it myself."

They were married on St. Valentine's Day, 1922, in Palm Beach. They also had their first public quarrel that day. The wedding was scheduled for 4 P.M., and when General MacArthur arrived he found his wife-to-be perched on a stepladder putting finishing touches to the decorations. He gave her a hearty lecture on preparedness. Nobody had ever spoken to her like that before. It did not go down very well.

Two months after the wedding General Pershing ordered MacArthur back to the Philippines. Washington had it that Pershing was so irked by the marriage that he was deliberately sending MacArthur into "exile." Pershing's only answer to this charge was "ridiculous." However, the ebullient, beautiful Mrs. Douglas MacArthur, who loved parties and the accouterments of the society merry-go-round to which she was accustomed, was not expected to fit very well into military life. Washington expected her to stand Manila about six months. They sailed for the Philippines with the two Brooks children as the newspapers hailed their marriage in headlines which read: Marriage of Mars and Millions.

From the very outset it would appear that Mrs. Douglas MacArthur hated Manila. It certainly was not "exile" for her General husband. He was enthusiastic about his return to the Philippines; he intended to carry on where his father left off. What was exciting to her husband was extremely dull to Louise MacArthur. She hated the heat and the everyday life of Manila. And she found army life quite unbearable. General MacArthur disliked formal parties; she adored them. They rarely attended such functions.

Mrs. MacArthur became so bored that she actually

had herself commissioned as a policewoman. This dispatch from Manila appeared in a New York paper on June 27, 1924: "A notable figure in Manila society, recently commissioned a policewoman, made her first arrest today. She had asked for the appointment to aid in the prevention of cruelty to animals. She took into custody the driver of a *carromata* and charged him with abusing his horse."

Louise MacArthur was very much in love with the General, but she could not understand her husband's constant absorption in military matters. She began, therefore, a campaign to persuade General MacArthur to resign from the Army. This must have been an extremely trying time for MacArthur, for it was quite apparent to everybody that he returned the love of his wife with equal fervor. Yet resignation from the Army was out of the question for him. He did the next best thing: in 1925 he asked for a transfer from his beloved Philippines. This must have been a difficult decision. In the same year he was transferred to Atlanta. Here, for a time, Louise MacArthur was happy once again in the gay whirl of society.

The following year MacArthur was promoted to the rank of major general. This gave him another honor, for he was then, at forty-three, the youngest major general in the Army. He was also the most bored. That same year he was transferred to Baltimore as commander of the Third Corps Area. This was more agreeable to him, for he was nearer the hub of the Army at Washington. Here, for the first time, he heard the malicious Washington gossips' latest piece of scandal: that his wife had been responsible for the promotion. To a marriage that seemed doomed to eventual dissolution this news sounded a telling blow.

The MacArthurs remained in Baltimore three years, maintaining an apartment in the city and a country estate in Greenspring Valley. Louise continued to press the General to resign, but he would hear none of it. This situation continued until MacArthur was ordered back to the Philippines in September of 1928. Mrs. MacArthur also left—for Reno.

They were divorced on June 17, 1929. The complaint charged "failure to provide," and Mrs. MacArthur told reporters as she left the courtroom:

"General MacArthur and I were divorced because we were wholly incompatible to each other. I have the greatest respect and admiration for him and we part as friends."

In the Philippines the local papers felt embarrassed about printing news of the divorce, and MacArthur gave them full authority to treat it as they would any other story.

This episode had been a trying one in the General's career. There had been no children of the marriage and MacArthur was left with nothing but a rather bitter memory. He had made many concessions, whether through love or duty, and so had Louise. Those who knew Mrs. MacArthur well during that period say that she was deeply in love with her soldier-husband, but she just was not "Army" and could not adapt herself to MacArthur's studious way of life, his constant and consuming love for anything dealing with matters military. In her own words the marriage had been "incompatible."

It is interesting to note that the General's mother at no time during their marriage passed an opinion on her daughter-in-law. Indeed Mary MacArthur, for reasons best known to herself, remained in the background during the seven years of her son's marriage.

In 1930 the former Mrs. MacArthur became the wife of Lionel Atwill, the actor. He had been married twice before and was at that time one of the most sought-after character actors in Hollywood. This marriage lasted thirteen years; they were divorced on June 17, 1943.

It was during her marriage to Atwill that Louise became active in politics. Drew Pearson, in 1940, called her "one of the most popular women in Washington" when he reported that a "powerful one-lady lobby is being staged by Mrs. Lionel Atwill." This activity was to press for the appointment for a certain Mr. Ashurst as a judge. After the Senate debate Vice-President Alben Barkley (then a senator) said to her: "Listen, Mickey Mouse, I thought I saw two bright eyes back in the Senate gallery when Vandenberg objected." Washington saw a lot of Mrs. Atwill during that period, but her lobbying was of no avail.

She was to come into the limelight again with the opening of the Pacific struggle. As MacArthur made his gallant stand in the Philippines, hundreds of hysterical people wrote letters to her condemning her for having divorced the General. They had been divorced fifteen years at this time, and General MacArthur had married again.

"Some of the letters were rather irritating," she said. "I was berated for having divorced such a wonderful hero. One letter, in particular, was downright threatening. It said that I had better do something about myself, because MacArthur was coming home and was going to run for the presidency. And that no man could have two living wives and be president, so one wife would have to be bumped off. I guess that meant me."

Newspapers and syndicates telephoned from all over the country offering her large sums for stories about her former husband.

"One of them even wanted to purchase the General's love letters for a large amount," she said. "I had all those letters locked up, because they were so beautiful. Of course I didn't sell them."

As MacArthur was tossed into further dramatic situations in the Pacific the more threatening became the letters to Mrs. Atwill. Finally she appealed to the FBI. They told her not to worry. "Edgar Hoover told me, however, not to open any large packages that ticked."

She married for the fourth time in 1944 Captain Alfred Heiberg, an air force officer five years her junior.

The newspapers never forgot that she was once Mrs. Douglas MacArthur, and in 1948, when the Mac-Arthur-for-President boom was on, she confessed that her former husband was not her idea of a presidential candidate. "If he's a dark horse," she said, "he's in the last roundup."

Jean Faircloth MacArthur, the General's second wife, is the direct antithesis of the first. She loves the Army, feels and acts part of it, and is completely devoted to her husband and their twelve-year-old son, Arthur. Through cold and hot wars she has been by her husband's side, and today she is once again right in the thick of things. At the opening of World War II she was in Manila when the first bombs dropped; this time she was with her famous husband in their home in Tokyo when the first shots were fired in Korea only a few hundred miles away. Jean MacArthur likes it that way; like General MacArthur, who adores the ground she walks on, she has always had a penchant for anything military.

They were married on April 30, 1937, in the chapel of the New York City Municipal Building. It was a very quiet affair—so quiet, in fact, that her family knew nothing about it.

Remembering the embarrassing publicity of his first ultra-fashionable wedding, MacArthur went to great pains to keep his second marriage very simple. There were few reporters present. The General on this occasion even abandoned his magnificent dress uniform, wearing, instead, a quiet brown civilian suit; Jean wore brown too.

There was no fanfare about this wedding. MacArthur would not give an interview but did remark that "this job is going to last a long time." Then directly after the ceremony they left for the Waldorf-Astoria and a wedding breakfast of ham and eggs. The next day they were on their way to Manila. Neither of them has been back to the United States since.

Jean Faircloth's family was astonished at the news. Although she had talked about MacArthur and referred to him as "the General," she had not given a hint of the romance. But the news was not a surprise to ailing Mary MacArthur, the General's mother—she had arranged the match. It was the last gesture she was to perform for her son. She had stood by his side throughout his whole career. She had heard him acclaimed for his courage and leadership in World War I; she had also heard him castigated as an "alarmist" and a "warmonger" while he was Chief of Staff. She was not to live to see her son's greatest triumphs; to hear him acclaimed and criticized in the same breath. It seems an irony that this woman who had developed by her love and indomitable character a great leader for the Army should unknowingly be failed in her last hours by the very service her life had been dedicated to. MacArthur appealed to Washington for a special serum which might have saved, or at least prolonged, her life. It arrived too late. She died only a few days before the clipper landed at Manila.

Whether because of temperament or eccentricity MacArthur has always needed an anchor. His mother provided it while she lived; she left Jean Faircloth that responsibility when she died. "He is going to love you very much," she told the future Mrs. MacArthur. She was right.

The tiny brunette—she weighs only a hundred pounds—with the flashing smile whom MacArthur had taken as his bride was born in the southern college town of Murfreesboro, Tennessee. Her parents were divorced when she was quite young. Her mother, "Miss Sally," remarried. Jean had three brothers and a sister. From all accounts it was a gay, happy family. And the children's greatest pleasure was when they gathered in the parlor— a typical Victorian room with a glass-enclosed clock on the mantel, a cello in the corner—and sang around the piano.

The family lived in a two-story white house with an imposing white pillared portico. It was for the most part spacious and old-fashioned with large rooms filled with paintings—from full-length portraits to miniatures— of military scenes, battles, and military heroes. The house was run by a colored "Mammy" who had a hand of iron and a heart of gold. "About the only thing we ever saw of Miss Jean," Mammy Dromgoole once complained, "was her coattails." Her early beaux complained, too, that "only a fellow in uniform will marry Jean."

Jean seemed to have prepared all her life to be a sol-

dier's wife. She was immensely proud of her grandfather, Richard Beard, who had been a Confederate
captain. She was a Daughter of the Confederacy and
a Daughter of the American Revolution. She was
known as the "flag-wavingest girl in Murfreesboro."
And it was said that "every time Jean Marie heard a
Fourth-of-July firecracker go off, she jumped to attention."

Even her formal education prepared her to be a soldier's wife. She went to a small private academy named
Soule and then spent a year at Ward-Belmont College
in Nashville, Tennessee.

Murfreesboro (population, 10,000) loved Jean and
she loved Murfreesboro. The town used to be the capital
of Tennessee. There is a courthouse with a red brick
tower, a Confederate monument in the square where the
farmers meet each week when they come to town, and a
red cedar bucket factory that makes churns and wine
coolers. Add to this Jean's own father's flour mill and a
chain of bakeries (he later added banking to his activities) and one has a picture of the town Jean grew up in.
She was always loyal to Murfreesboro. Right up until
Pearl Harbor she ordered all her cosmetics and maga-
zines from her favorite drugstore in town and had them
shipped to Manila. Her clothes she had sent from a department store in Nashville.

Jean was always particularly fond of her father, and
he seemed to look upon her with deep affection. He enjoyed spending money on her and she never lacked anything she wanted. She enjoyed traveling more than
anything else and went on several sea cruises with her
father. And while he was not a particularly rich man, at
his death he left Jean an inheritance of more than $200,-
000. Almost immediately she began traveling, and in

October 1935 she left for a long vacation in Shanghai. On board the S.S. *Hoover* en route to the Far East she met her future husband.

General MacArthur was then on his way to organize the Philippine Army and to put into force his ten-year plan for the defense of the islands. His mother met Jean on board and introduced her to the General. At first MacArthur seemed to take little interest. He was too deeply involved in making plans for the army he was about to set up and spent most of the trip in consultation with his officers. He was only seen at mealtimes. Furthermore, he was extremely worried about the health of his mother, who had been ailing for some time. His mother didn't seem to be worrying too much about that; she was busily matchmaking. The more she got to know Jean the more she hoped that her son would one day marry her.

There were many things in Jean's favor. She was from the South; so was Mrs. MacArthur. She had a lively and appealing personality, a quick smile, and was an easy conversationalist; she was chic and pretty, and, above everything else—as far as Mary Pinkney Hardy MacArthur was concerned—she loved the Army.

Mrs. MacArthur prevailed upon Jean to continue on to Manila with her and see the inauguration of Manuel Quezon, the Philippine President, who was also on the liner. Jean agreed, and instead of the long visit she had planned, spent only a night or two in Shanghai and then went on to Manila, where she stayed for a year and a half. It was during this period that the romance between Jean Faircloth and Douglas MacArthur blossomed.

She returned to Murfreesboro in the spring of 1937. But while she mentioned MacArthur, she gave no hint of her plans. She spent only a few weeks there, and then told her friends she was going away to visit an aunt in Louisville, Kentucky. She stayed a night in Louisville and then continued on to New York. MacArthur left Manila and quietly arrived in New York. Shortly thereafter they were married.

In Manila they lived in the beautiful air-conditioned penthouse apartment atop the new six-story Manila Hotel. Unlike the first Mrs. MacArthur, Jean became a success overnight with the small army group of wives. Her naturalness, her very lack of superficiality endeared her to everybody. To most army wives it is politic to "like" the general's wife. But with Jean MacArthur it was different: she was genuinely loved by all ranks— particularly by her husband, who began to lose some of his austerity. Indeed she is credited with "humanizing" the aloof MacArthur. In a sense she gave him confidence in himself; this is difficult to understand perhaps, but MacArthur has always had an inherent shyness, afraid to unbend. He once said that "a general's life is loneliness." It wasn't with the new Mrs. MacArthur.

Always a studious man, who spent hours in his 7,000-volume library, MacArthur found that his wife was just as much at home with things military as he was. In those happier days they entertained quite a lot. They preferred intimate dinner parties, and just as now they both disliked large social gatherings. They found that they both had one great weakness: movies. To this day they both have that failing, and the proud, dignified, aloof General who has so often been accused of "being above everybody else" has a real passion for cowboy movies—good or bad. Recently a friend of the family had this to say on the subject: "It's sure kind of the General to invite us to see his movies, but sometimes I wish

I could refuse. I've sat through his favorite cowboy picture ten times already."

In 1938 their only son, Arthur MacArthur, was born. The arrival of the new MacArthur to carry on the heritage of a great military family was the greatest single event in MacArthur's life. He had unbent a great deal when he remarried, but those close to him say that he became a "softie" with the arrival of Arthur MacArthur.

The myth of MacArthur rarely takes into the picture the fact that the General is just as natural as anybody else, and makes as many mistakes as the average person. The legend hardly includes this story which began before Corregidor.

At about seven-thirty each morning the door of the General's room was thrown open and in marched "Sergeant" Arthur MacArthur, aged three. The General immediately snapped to attention. Then followed a series of snappy salutes. The General then marched around the room with the sergeant following to the "sounding off" of Boom! Boom! Boomity Boom! The game always ended with Arthur receiving a small gift, such as a crayon, funny paper, a piece of candy, or some other trifle. Then, as the General shaved, the sergeant formed the junior member of a singing duet. MacArthur once told a group of friends on the subject of his singing: "The fact of the matter is that the only person who appreciates my singing in the bathroom is Arthur." Recently, when the boy gave his father a water color which he had specially painted for the General's birthday, MacArthur told everyone that "this is better than a Rembrandt." For Arthur MacArthur, called after his famous grandfather, is the apple of his father's eye.

Mrs. MacArthur has always remained in the background. Some people feel that her husband deliberately keeps her there. The consensus in Tokyo is that Jean MacArthur cleverly remains out of the limelight for no other reason but the desire for privacy. She remained by her husband's side throughout the Pacific war. This included Corregidor, when with her husband she refused to take refuge in the huge subterranean tunnels. In a little house perched on the side of the fortress they lived through one air raid after another. The nurses and soldiers on the "Rock" loved little Arthur. "Hello, little general," one of the soldiers called one day. Arthur replied, "I am not a general; I am a sergeant." After Corregidor MacArthur gave his wife a watch with the words "to my bravest" inscribed on the back.

When she returned to the Philippines, a storm of criticism arose. Why, asked the wives of other army men, should Mrs. MacArthur be different than anybody else? Washington gave this answer: "If feminine companionship serves in any way to help MacArthur, let her stay there. MacArthur is not a young man. Maybe he needs his wife." Those close to them say that the General certainly does need her. He seems at times completely lost without her. Even when they were in Australia for two and a half years, Mrs. MacArthur cooked all his meals. They were as inseparable then as they are today. He never forgets her. At the end of the war she returned to Manila and there over the radio heard her husband speaking from the broad deck of the battleship *Missouri*, commanding the Japanese emissaries to sign away fifteen years of aggression. MacArthur signed for the Allied nations with five different pens. One of them, a small, cheap red pen, he later returned to its owner—Mrs. MacArthur.

Today they live in the fifteen-year-old granite embassy building in Tokyo atop the rolling Renanzaka

hillside overlooking the rubble of the city. Jean Mac-
Arthur still calls him "the General" or, occasionally,
humorously, "Sir Boss," just as she did when they were
first married. He still calls her "ma'am," and Arthur is
still the "sergeant." They live elegantly and quietly. Few
people have been allowed to see the inside of the embassy other than the living room and dining room. The
MacArthurs have tried—especially for the sake of their
son—to keep their home life as private as possible.

Their life has not changed much since the Manila
days with the one exception that the General works
longer hours. He keeps a rigid, unbending schedule. He
rises at seven and breakfasts with his wife (orange juice,
toast, and hot chocolate, two eggs boiled one minute
into which he mixes butter and pepper), reads his mail
and a condensation of world news. Promptly at nine he
leaves for the office and returns at one for lunch. This
meal is served by eight Japanese servants who wear
chocolate-brown kimonos with the United States seal
emblazoned on them. Lunch generally lasts two and a
half hours, and directly after MacArthur returns to his
headquarters at the Dai Ichi Building and works until
about seven-thirty. His day generally ends with a movie.

Jean MacArthur has injected a gay atmosphere into
the rather gloomy embassy building. It is a magnificent
mansion which cost nearly a million dollars to make it
earthquake proof. Mrs. MacArthur redecorated the in-
terior, and the principal room—the living room—is a
blaze of color. Japanese kimonos and obis cover the
walls. The floors are deeply carpeted, and every nook
and cranny holds jeweled cigarette boxes, lacquered
fans, and hand-beaten silver which Mrs. MacArthur
collects. There are delicately painted screens, huge paintings, and enormous quantities of flowers in every room.

The MacArthurs now have all their belongings in the embassy, but the General's priceless collection of books which made up his 7,000-volume library was lost during the destruction of Manila. However, he has collected fifteen trunks of documents from which one day it is hoped he will write his autobiography.

Young Arthur MacArthur is the real focal point of their lives. He is a strangely serious boy who speaks with a slight British accent, probably as a result of his British governess. He has never seen his homeland, but he has been closer to the making of its history than many another child of his age. He is an avid reader—the first book he read was a child's history of Robert E. Lee— and a promising musician. Already he has composed two pieces for the piano.

MacArthur admits to pampering the boy but has sheltered him from all publicity, insisting that "the boy must be given a chance to grow up normally." Perhaps one of the reasons the MacArthurs would like to return to the United States is because of Arthur's education. Just before the Korean crisis an exchange of letters took place between General MacArthur and the board of Remington Rand; they offered the General a position with a salary of $100,000 per year. MacArthur is rumored to have accepted the post "if and when" he can return. As it is, the possibility is now very remote. "If I returned," he has since said, "for only a few weeks, word would spread through the Pacific that the United States is abandoning the Orient."

One day they may return, for, as Mrs. MacArthur puts it, "Well, we are Americans, you know." The Mac-Arthurs today find themselves once more serving their country in another crisis; it is doubtful if they will even think of returning until that crisis is over. "As long as I have the strength to continue and my government wants me to continue, so long shall I stay on the job," MacArthur recently said. However, Mrs. MacArthur will probably make the final decision, for on the matter of "decisions" her husband has said: "Any husband will tell you that the wife absolutely rules the family."

4. MacArthur in World War I

"All right, gentlemen, after me," said the young brigadier general. Whistles shrilled up and down the line. Doughboys poured out of front-line trenches and dashed across the muddy death-filled wilderness of no man's land. Out in front "The Dude," as the thirty-eight-year-old General was good-naturedly called, dashed ahead. His men crouched over their rifles, brought the steel brims of their helmets lower over their eyes. The General carried only a swagger stick; had never worn a helmet. But his famous drooping hat had been given an extra tilt. It now hung even more rakishly over one eye. That same hat had caused the late Floyd Gibbons to comment that "The tilt permits his personality to emerge without violating army regulations."

Now it bobbed up and down as the General led the thin line of men into the attack. A few hours later a runner came panting into the brigade headquarters with a message. "It's from the General," he said. The note read: "Entered Essey at 10:45 A.M. Bridge intact. Troops already across the river . . . We have picked up several hundred prisoners as well as a number of guns . . . Communicate direct to the Chief of Staff . . . tell him confidentially for me that this is the life." It was signed MacArthur.

That was the first time that young General Douglas MacArthur had been given a chance to command a brigade in World War I, and the Germans never forgot it. MacArthur leading the 84th Infantry Brigade of the Rainbow Division (the famous 42nd) cut a crack Prussian Guard unit to pieces and then continued the advance.

But it had been a long haul. The boy who heard the twang of the Indian bow in New Mexico heard the swish of a glittering bolo knife and the whine of an enemy bullet for the first time in the Philippines. In his own words Douglas MacArthur was "just a young shavetail" fresh out of West Point in 1903 when he was ordered out to the islands.

He chose the engineers as his branch of the service, the Philippines as the place to get into action as soon as possible. In the islands the American forces were still busy mopping up insurgent bands; down on the island of Mindanao Captain John J. ("Black Jack") Pershing had had his troubles in jungle warfare against the savage bolo-swinging Moros.

His father's fine work among the Filipinos a few years before made Douglas welcome at Manila. He went to work as an engineer in a lush tropical setting; he cut roads through wilderness and around mountains, built piers and other facilities that were to give the people a start toward economic self-sufficiency.

On the island of Samar, one of the easternmost of the Philippines chain, a band of brigands known as "pulahanes" was pretty active. Young MacArthur was dispatched with a small detachment of regulars from the Philippine Department to clean them out. As he recalls the story—one of his favorites—"luck was with the MacArthurs, out here, from the beginning."

With his .38 caliber service pistol in hand, Mac-
Arthur, applying the Indian-stalking tactics that his
father had instilled, crept at the head of his group
through tangled undergrowth. Suddenly there was a
roar from a heavily loaded rebel shotgun. MacArthur's
orderly dropped beside him, half of his face shot off.
MacArthur bent over his dying comrade. It was lucky
he did so, for a second charge, aimed at his breast, ripped
through his pinched-crown campaign hat and tore it
from his head. With a wild shout the rebels swung out
of trees and leafy green hideouts swinging razor-sharp
knives. MacArthur concedes that he may have been a
trifle pale around the gills. As he and his men fired away
at the foe from prone positions a gruff old sergeant
crawled alongside, handed MacArthur his tattered hat,
and remarked: "With the lieutenant's kind permission,
may I remark that the rest of the lieutenant's life is now
on velvet?"

MacArthur had other narrow escapes against the
natives, but much as he loved action, there is nothing
in the available record to show that he echoed George
Washington's letter to his mother: "I heard the bullets
whistle, and believe me, there is something charming in
the sound."

The young soldier remained in the Philippines for
about a year, returning in 1904. In 1905 Russia and
Japan were at war, and Douglas MacArthur's father,
Lieutenant General Arthur MacArthur, was assigned
by President Theodore Roosevelt to head a group of
American officers attached as observers to the Japanese
Army. The General took along his son, now a first lieu-
tenant, after a stiff going over by an examining board.

It was MacArthur's first experience of the Japanese—
as well as of the Russians. He never forgot the fanaticism

of either or their disregard of human beings. He watched the Japs in a weird mass suicide at the battle of the Yalu River. The Japs were winning; the Russians fighting a withdrawal to the river. Japanese headquarters ordered a brigade that had chased the Russians to the water's edge to pull back. The puzzled Nipponese foot soldiers interpreted the order as a sign of disgrace. Rather than lose face, they fell upon their swords, 1,000 at a time.

Douglas MacArthur also saw the tremendous Battle of Mukden and actually went into combat on the Japanese side. Six times he watched the Japanese charge a Russian-held hill; six times they were driven off. MacArthur couldn't stand it. He dashed across country, spurred on the Japanese troops, and took them up the hill to victory.

In 1906 Douglas MacArthur was back in the United States. He became military aide to President Theodore Roosevelt. In 1914 we were having trouble with Mexico; MacArthur joined up with Major General Frederick Funston on the expedition that occupied Vera Cruz. MacArthur got himself up as a Mexican tramp, slipped behind the Mexican lines, and located three locomotives for his chief. He had some help from a young official of the German Legation named Franz von Papen, later a German spy and saboteur in the United States, and in World War II an agent procovateur, disguised as a diplomat, for the Nazis.

All this was, in one sense, an apprenticeship for the Western Front of World War I. When it began, MacArthur somehow sensed that a world war might be in the offing and he didn't want to miss it. He received his majority in 1915 and persuaded his superiors to put him on the General Staff in Washington. He talked himself into a staff job—chief of censors—which he was to loathe later on. For a professional soldier who loved the excitement of war, this post was not calculated to increase the beating of his pulse. Furthermore, he was out of uniform and into civilian dress. Now he was tied to a desk censoring copy.

It was even harder to take when the United States declared war in 1917. For four anxious months MacArthur tried everything in order to be transferred from the General Staff to duty with the troops. Then one day the Secretary of War, Newton D. Baker, sent for him. MacArthur, who might be termed Baker's protégé, had decided that he would put his case before his chief. This was going to be the opportunity. He did not know, at the time, that Baker had been thinking about him too.

As he entered Baker's office the Secretary seemed to be daydreaming. Then he looked up and said: "Major, what do you think of the idea of creating a division out of the National Guard units of the entire forty-eight states?"

"The idea's great!" MacArthur replied with enthusiasm. "It will spread over the country—like a rainbow."

"That's what we'll call it," said Baker; "the Rainbow Division."

What MacArthur did not know was that nearly every senior officer had turned down the idea. The name sparked the idea so greatly in Baker's mind that it clinched the decision. Five days later, on August 5, 1917, MacArthur was given a colonelcy and made Chief of Staff of the new division under General Mann. In Baker's office MacArthur had been so excited over the new division that he had forgotten to plead his case to go overseas.

December 7 is an important date in MacArthur's life. He officially went to war in 1917 on that date when the last troops of the Rainbow Division landed in France. Another December 7, twenty-four years later, was to throw him into another war—a war he had foreseen and warned the nation about when he was Chief of Staff of the Rainbow Division. His prophecies went unheeded; he was thanked with the jibes and sneers of a Congress whose only thought was to disband and disarm. Just as with Churchill, MacArthur's was a voice in the wilderness in the years between.

But here we find MacArthur, at the age of thirty-seven, training his troops in the bitter cold of a French winter. MacArthur was the division's first member, but with him he had proud units from twenty-six states and the District of Columbia: machine-gun companies from Wisconsin, Pennsylvania, and Georgia; artillerymen from Illinois, Indiana, Minnesota, Maryland, and Kansas; engineers from North Carolina, South Carolina, and California; military police and headquarters troops from Virginia and Louisiana; medics, hospital, and ambulance units from the District of Columbia, Michigan, Nebraska, New Jersey, Tennessee, Oklahoma, Oregon, and Colorado; signal corps men from Missouri; supply train from Texas; infantrymen from New York, Iowa, Alabama, and Ohio. This was the Rainbow Division, and as the adjutant of the 84th Brigade (soon to be led by MacArthur) wrote of it:

"To every person the symbol of the rainbow suggests the same idea in a different way. The many states of the Union, the many types of life, the many colors and shades of thought and points of view that were all brought together in the 42nd Division in a new camp in New York in the fall of 1917 were as contrasting, as carefully blended, as strong, and as far-reaching as the rainbow, which, for always, has epitomized the beauty and strength of union and the endlessness of union—foɪ who has ever found the end of the rainbow?—as well as the constancy of hope, which will alone bring victory."

Besides MacArthur, out of that division were to come two other famous characters—Father Duffy and Colonel "Wild Bill" Donovan. In World War II "Wild Bill" of the old "Fighting 69th" was to become chief of the "Cloak and Dagger" boys—the OSS.

MacArthur breathed a sigh of relief when the last man of the division landed in France. As Chief of Staff he was naturally responsible for all the arrangements of organization and transportation. The transportation of the division across the stormy wintry Atlantic was a nightmare all of itself. Five days out of port the S.S. *President Grant,* carrying the 168th Infantry, had to drop out of the convoy and turn back, without escort, for New York. Transferred to the S.S. *Celtic,* the troops were only a few days out of Halifax when the harbor was blasted by one of the worst port explosions in recorded history. All this was just a preamble to the hardships and dangers awaiting the men of the 42nd at the front.

To his men MacArthur was known as the "Beau Brummell of the 42nd," or the "Fighting Dude." Always nattily dressed, his great weakness seemed to lie then, as it does now, in hats. In France one of the first things he did was to remove the grommet, or wire strengthener, from the inside of his hat, thus giving it a droopy, rakish appearance. Once he was asked why he never wore a helmet. He replied: "I haven't got time to change my headgear." He never wore a helmet during any phase of the Pacific war either. In World War I he was warned that he would be "picked off" because of his famous hat, and oddly enough the same fear was expressed by an officer in World War II when Mac-Arthur visited an island where the fighting was still in progress. One of his staff, noticing that the General's unique gold-braided hat was glinting in the sun, offered a helmet, saying, "Excuse me, sir, but we killed a sniper in there just a few minutes ago." MacArthur, appearing not to notice the proffered helmet, said, "Fine; that's the best thing to do with them," and stalked off into the jungle. Recently, when he visited the front lines in Korea, he was once more without a helmet, and the gold-braided cap was just as battered as the field cap he wore on the Western Front in World War I.

He had a passion for four-yard mufflers, raccoon coats, plum ties, high roll-necked sweaters, and crisp, perfectly cut riding breeches. There was something about young Douglas in World War I reminiscent of George S. Patton in the second, at least as far as dressing was concerned. Patton could walk through the muddiest field and still appear sartorially perfect; Mac-Arthur was just as fastidious. Both generals had a weakness for highly polished riding boots.

In those early days of training MacArthur would appear with his four-yard muffler wrapped around his throat again and again and the end tossed nonchalantly over one shoulder. Gripped in his teeth would be a long, fancy jeweled cigarette holder. He was more partial to cigarettes than corncobs in those days.

The division headquarters was situated at the town of La Franche far from the front. Here in this quiet sector life was quite normal. Staff officers slept in beds and fought a "gentleman's war." But MacArthur hadn't been in France a week before he began to pester the General for duty at the front line. Aging General Mann, who was later to be replaced by General Menoher, had a difficult time holding MacArthur back. But when General Menoher took over, just before the 42nd was committed to the front lines, MacArthur begged, pleaded, and finally got permission to make an "inspection tour" of the front. The General must have often wondered why his Chief of Staff had been so insistent on making an "inspection tour" to acquaint himself with trench warfare at that particular time. The real answer was that MacArthur had heard of a raid the French were planning in the vicinity of Réchicourt and he wanted to be in on it. Turning over his duties to a couple of assistants, he left camp with two close friends, muffler flying in the wind, bejeweled cigarette holder in his mouth.

The "D'Artagnan of the Western Front," as he was later to be called, found himself some nights later in a dark trench at the front rubbing heavy, sticky black mud over his face, for this was going to be a commando raid of the quiet knife-sticking variety. It was bitterly cold and raining hard. A French lieutenant briefed him on trench-raid tactics, offered him a pair of wire clippers and a trench knife. This was a relatively quiet sector of the front, but occasionally a machine gun chattered, while far off the booming of big guns told of action on some other part of the front. MacArthur refused the trench knife, and when they crawled over the top he had no weapon other than his swagger stick.

Very lights burst over them as they moved quietly through the shell-pitted darkness of no man's land. The flares hung in the air, outlining the whole sour face of the battleground: the twisted barbed wire leaning on crazily bent poles; the water-filled shell holes and the oozing mud. The party silently moved up to the first

lines of barbed wire and cut their way through. The
signal for the attack was to be the explosion of a grenade
thrown by one of the French poilus. They reached the
German wire and snipped through that, then they
waited, face down in the mud, for the explosion of the
grenade.

Somewhere ahead there was a blinding flash and a
roar. Immediately they were on their feet running
toward the first German trench. Like black specters they
dived into the confusion of the startled Germans. All
along the front in the immediate vicinity machine guns
started to rattle nervously. Rifles opened fire, and more
flares shot up into the inky rain of the black night. In
the close confines of the trench the French party pant-
ingly fought hand to hand with the Germans. Mac-
Arthur, with some others, fought his way down into a
dugout and prodded a few Germans out, over the top,
and back through the gap in the barbed wire as prisoners. Then they were out again, and the raid was over.
But they had to get back. By this time the Germans
knew what had happened. Machine guns ripped close
to the ground just over the heads of the attackers and
their prisoners. Inch by inch they crawled back to their
own trenches, dodging from one shell hole to another.
One last dash, and they dived headlong into French
trenches. When a count was made there was no sign of
MacArthur. But he showed up later, prodding a very
muddy and incensed German colonel at the end of his
swagger stick. In the process MacArthur had lost his
title as the 42nd's Beau Brummell, for the dashing young
colonel had left the seat of his impeccably cut riding
breeches on the barbed wire.

MacArthur's first raid was soon the talk of the 42nd—
especially the part about his breeches. The French

Seventh Army honored him with the Croix de Guerre for his feat. General Menoher dryly complimented him on his "inspection tour of the front." A fellow officer felt that as Chief of Staff of the division, MacArthur should not have exposed himself to such risks. "Why did you do it?" he is reported to have asked. MacArthur replied: "It's all in the game."

A few days later the 42nd was committed to a "quiet" sector of the line. Full-scale offensives in the area were considered impractical by both sides—at least so the French said. The area may have been "quiet" in the preceding months, but when the 42nd took over things began to happen. In the next few weeks the Rainbow Division suffered heavy casualties from constant shelling and gas attack. It was during this period that Mac-Arthur himself fell a victim to the gas of the enemy.

Ten days after taking up positions at the front the 167th Infantry was ordered to raid a heavily defended wood known as Bois des Feyes. At the headquarters at Baccarat, some fifteen miles back, MacArthur once more relinquished his staff duties to his assistants and headed for the front. It was the 42nd's first raid and MacArthur wanted to be in on it; it was quite a surprise to the doughboys when their Chief of Staff led them over the top.

He took off his heavy overcoat just before zero hour and threw it in a thicket, then personally led the attack. The Germans shelled the troops heavily, as the infantry moved forward, and included in the barrage several gas shells. One of them exploded near the thicket and saturated MacArthur's overcoat. After the raid, when he picked up his coat, he was severely gassed from the impregnated cloth.

General Menoher had this to say about MacArthur

in that raid: "He accompanied the assaulting wave of the American companies engaged with the sole view of lending his presence where it was reassuring to the troops who were then unaccustomed to this manner of endeavor. On this occasion, in the face of the determined and violent resistance of an alert enemy, he lent actual service on the spot to the unit commanders and by his supervision of the operation not only guaranteed its success, but left the division with the knowledge of the constant attention of their leaders to their problems in action and the sense of security which the wise and courageous leadership there impressed on the engaged companies." MacArthur won the D.S.C. for this episode.

The next four months found MacArthur recuperating from gas poisoning but still active at headquarters. Indeed it has been said that he hardly stayed in the hospital at all. However, on his return to duty as Chief of Staff a greater control was exercised over his movements, for his exploits were not looked upon with great favor by his seniors. In fact, there were those who thought he was a little "irresponsible." But active soldiering was the type the MacArthurs—both father and son—had always reveled in. MacArthur yearned to be at the front.

He was promoted to the rank of brigadier general in June 1918. It was about this time that the Rainbow Division moved out of the "quiet" sector, having made a record for itself for holding one front longer than any other unit while under extremely heavy fire. It was put back into combat in July, when it relieved the 26th Division in the sector commanded by the famed French General Gouraud, and his order of the day just before the Germans threw everything into the last final push will always be remembered by the men of the 42nd.

"To the French and American soldiers of the Fourth

Army: We may be attacked at any moment. You all know that a defensive battle was never engaged under more favorable conditions. We are awake and on our guard. We are powerfully reinforced with infantry and artillery. The bombardment will be terrific. You will stand it without tremor. The assault will be fierce, in a cloud of smoke, dust, and gas. But your positions and your armament are formidable. In your breasts beat the brave, strong hearts of free men. None shall look to the rear; none shall yield a step. Each shall have but one thought: to kill, to kill aplenty, until they have had their fill. Therefore your general says to you: you will break the assault and it will be a happy day."

The attack came on July 14, 1918. For five hours, starting at midnight, Allied positions along a fifty-mile front pivoted at Reims were raked with shell fire. Then just before dawn the Germans left their trenches. The Rainbow Division and the French in their sector were hit by a crack Prussian Guard division, the 1st and 2nd Bavarian and the 30th and 72nd divisions. Six assaults were made, and six times they were thrown back. The entire German offensive was smashed within six days.

It was during this battle that MacArthur really made a name for himself. In the town of Sergy, at the height of the fighting, an ambulance rattled along through the mud. Standing on the running board was Brigadier General MacArthur. The town had just been captured and MacArthur was eager to determine just how fast the Germans were retreating. What he saw convinced him that this was the propitious time to attack. For the Germans were not only retreating in confusion but it seemed that they were pulling out of prepared positions even farther back. MacArthur rushed back to division headquarters and begged General Menoher to attack.

Menoher, conscious that his men had been fighting six nights and days, at first said no. "Every unit," he told MacArthur, "is tired out, dead on their feet." But MacArthur persisted, and finally Menoher agreed. Without written orders MacArthur organized and led the attack.

General Menoher wrote of MacArthur and this action: "At the end of this phase of the division's employment, when it had labored night and day for a week, and was brought low in numbers by vigorous resistance to the assaults from exceptionally powerful positions, occurred an example of leadership and the high qualities of command which I consider unique. General MacArthur, himself on the advanced line of command at a time when the American First Army Corps had not ordered the division to advance, accurately diagnosed the situation as one in which the enemy had but one hour before broken contact. In advance of orders and without delay, he, with my concurrence, at an early hour organized the entire division into prompt pursuit which soon brought him on the very heels of the enemy and gained entire possession of the great massif of the Fôret de Nesselers, sparing a fresh division from the labors of penetration of this large territory and leaving its full force available for a running relief at the end of which it would be free to deliver the full weight of its blow."

Quick thinking and the spirited response of a tired but game division won for MacArthur an oak leaf to his Distinguished Service Cross and resulted in the command of a brigade, the 84th (Alabama and Iowa Infantry) in September.

On September 12, during the Saint-Mihiel offensive, in which American forces made their first shoulder-to-shoulder army attack, MacArthur advanced so rapidly that he sent a message back to brigade headquarters, which was situated, incidentally, on the very front lines ("I like it that way," he once told a friend; "it shortens my lines of communications"), ordering them to "pack up complete, trucks, motorcars, and motorcycles with all maximum speed possible to Essey, where I will have somebody there to meet them. . . . I myself will probably have moved forward to Pannes." When his headquarters reached Essey, the fighting General was miles ahead, so far ahead, in fact, that the chief of staff at General Foch's headquarters, a personal friend of MacArthur, asked him to stop on a certain line, as Foch himself was planning a concerted attack from that area. Foch's chief of staff was also worried in case MacArthur and his brigade tried to take the medievel German fortress of Metz. Here was enacted, by a strange coincidence, precisely what was to occur again twenty-six years later, in World War II.

In 1944 General Patton's tanks were breathing hot lead on the heels of the retreating Germans. Moving rapidly into the Valley of the Moselle, forward units crossed the river and came under the towering fortress guns of Metz. No shots were fired, so the commander of the unit entered the city which had only once before in its history been taken by frontal assault—by Napoleon. Surrounding the city were eight forts with hydraulic guns of 1914–18 vintage, which, after each shot, disappeared down into massive concrete emplacements. The guns, with stacks of heavy-caliber shells beside them, had been left by fleeing gun crews in perfect condition. Patton's tanks, cautiously patrolling, found that the enemy had long since fled. Control of Metz meant control of the surrounding heights and the Valley of the Moselle. But because Patton was "too far extended" he was ordered to pull out. Four months later Patton's United States Third Army suffered the greatest number of casualties in its entire campaign in retaking the citadel.

In 1918 MacArthur could have taken the great German fortress but he, too, was restrained because he was "extended beyond his limits." MacArthur and indeed many other strategists have repeatedly said since that had Metz been taken the extrication of the German armies from the Western Front might have been prevented, and this, in turn, might have caused complete defeat.

On the night of September 12 MacArthur and his troops entered the town of Saint-Benoît just as the last trainload of troops was pulling out. Establishing himself in the hundred-room Château Saint-Benoît, the former German headquarters, MacArthur was surprised to get a message from division headquarters which caustically informed him to "keep away from the Château Saint-Benoît, the Germans have mined it." Later, when he was asked why he had not heeded the message, he said: "The German headquarters troops set fire to the château just before they left and we put it out. They would hardly have set fire to the place if they had mined it, now would they?"

MacArthur remained in the château for ten days, during which time he conducted several raids in conjunction with the Meuse-Argonne offensive which was then under way. He was slightly wounded during this offensive but refused to be hospitalized. He left the château the day before the Germans demolished the building with heavy and continuous gunfire.

MacArthur's amazing sixth sense shows up throughout the whole of his career. There was one other gen-

eral who had this highly developed uncanny quality
—his name was Rommel. In other respects, too, there is
a strange comparison between the characters of both
men. Rommel's sixth sense (the Germans call it An-
schauungsvermögen) saved him time and time again.
Once when he was watching a tank battle in North
Africa he said to his aide: "Let's move over to that hill.
I feel that it is going to get warm around here pretty
soon." They moved to the hill, which was situated a
hundred yards away. Immediately thereafter the spot
they had been previously standing on was shelled continuously for fully ten minutes. On another occasion
Rommel announced to his staff officer that he intended
to evacuate his headquarters within the hour, as he felt
"in his bones" that it was going to be raided. They
moved a few miles away. That night British commandos
raided the former headquarters and found it empty.
MacArthur in World Wars I and II "sensed" situations
long before they happened. Both generals felt they would
never be killed in battle; that they were not destined to
die in that fashion. Rommel was murdered by the Nazis
for his part in the plot against Hitler's life.

However, on that night of September 22, 1918, Mac-
Arthur's sixth sense saved his life and the lives of the
headquarters troops with him. He established his headquarters in a nearby wood and continued his raids on the
enemy.

About this time General Menoher wrote to General
Pershing about MacArthur, saying that "The contribu-
tions made to our military establishment by the general
officer have already had far-reaching effects. He has
stood for the actual physical command of large bodies of
troops in battle—not for a day, but for days, and I believe he has actually commanded larger bodies of troops

in the line than any other officer in our army, with, in each instance, conspicuous success."

The war was nearing its close when MacArthur was wounded again. This occurred when he led his men into their own artillery fire. MacArthur had seen that the Germans were leaving the battlefield and attacked irrespective of the dangers. This wound kept him hospitalized a month and should have deterred him from any further active battlefield leadership. But back to the front lines he went. He slept with his men, ate with them, and shared their joys and sorrows. "He was a hell-to-breakfast baby," said one former 42nd soldier, "long and lean, who could spit nickels and chase Germans like any doughboy in the Rainbow Division." He was beloved by his men even though he was a strict army disciplinarian; never once was there a word of criticism, a jibe, or sneer, for MacArthur led his men into the worst danger and brought them back with the lowest casualties on the front.

The most often told story about MacArthur is of his assault of a hill which stood in the path of General Summerall's 5th Corps. The 42nd was given the objective and the division's top brigade commander was sent for. MacArthur suggested a night infantry attack from both flanks. General Summerall felt that a heavy artillery barrage was necessary first before the infantry attack. MacArthur, in typical style, insisted on doing it his way.

"If your method fails?" questioned General Summerall.

"I will expect the penalty," was MacArthur's answer, "but if I succeed?"

"I'll recommend a promotion," answered General Summerall.

MacArthur and the 42nd took the hill. But he refused to accept the promotion and asked that the division commander, General Menoher, be given an army corps as "the 42nd had won the promotion." The promotion was granted, and General Menoher became commander of the 6th Corps, but not before he had thanked MacArthur by commending him to General Pershing in a letter.

"I do not feel that I am free to assume another command," he wrote, "without recording the services rendered by General Douglas MacArthur. These services, rendered constantly for over a year, and in the large part amidst active operations in the field, have been so soundly, brilliantly, and loyally performed that in recognition of them I see only a fair appraisal of the example of energy, courage, and efficiency which General MacArthur has set for the 42nd Division and the entire Army in France. He has developed, combined, and applied the use of infantry and correlated arms with an effect on the enemy, a husband of his own forces and means, and a resourcefulness which no other American commander in the field has. His efforts have been untiring, uninterrupted, and without the least regard for his own personal safety at each of the many times when he felt his personal leadership required his presence in the midst of the struggle."

MacArthur's greatest honor was to come to him within the last week of the war, but first he had to be "captured" by his own troops. Leading his brigade toward Sedan in the final advance of the war, units of the 1st Division "captured" him and his officers. They could not believe that American troops could be as far ahead as they were and thought MacArthur and his officers were Germans in disguise. That same week, too, MacArthur became commander of the 42nd Division.

It was quite a signal honor for a young brigadier general of only thirty-eight. A few days later the war ended, and for MacArthur, though he did not know it at the time, the road ahead was to be a bitter one.

MacArthur left Europe firmly convinced that a future war would be a "war of motion." Long before the Germans pointed out the fallacy of "Maginot-line thinking" by turning it, MacArthur wrote: "At no place other than western Europe does there exist a definitely flankless line (the Alps at one end, the North Sea at the other) with populations on each side of it of such density and readiness for war as to man it solidly from end to end. In no other region of equal size does there exist the good roads necessary to support armies of the size that fought for four years in northwest France and Belgium. Moreover, modern improvements in certain offensive weapons and transportation equipment have immeasurably increased the power of maneuver and of speedy concentration, and so made more dangerous any adaptation of the cordon system of defense." When he left France in 1919, loaded down with decorations, he was a true soldier's soldier. Many years would elapse before this brilliant soldier would become the embittered soldier-statesman that the world was to love and hate with divided passion.

5. West Point and "the Hat"

General Douglas MacArthur has always had one weakness: hats. He arrived at West Point in his cadet days wearing a ten-gallon Stetson. During World War I he removed the wire stiffener and his field cap hung rakishly over one eye. Returning to the United States in 1919, MacArthur refused to purchase a new hat. He liked his old battered hat; he was rather sentimental about it too. "I can't be bothered fussing around with hats," he told a close friend; "I like this one." Years later, during the Pacific struggle, his scrambled-egg hat became famous the world over. The "Hat" meant MacArthur. Today he still wears it, and it is doubtful if he has more than one.

There are several versions as to how he came by this particular design. Some say—the great majority—that he designed it himself. Others tell this story: in the Philippines in 1938 MacArthur sent back to Washington for a new full-dress uniform for evening wear. About that time the full-dress uniform had been redesigned, and when MacArthur received it the scrambled-egg hat was included. According to the story MacArthur thought that this new hat was "regulation." He took a liking to it and has worn it ever since. Whatever the truth, in more than one way hats tell the story of Mac-Arthur's barometric change in character.

The callow youth arrived at the Academy with a Stetson. He lost that, and for the next four years he was trim and proper in a cadet's cap. Then came his first tour of duty in the Philippines. He wore a frontier cap. In Washington at the start of World War I, in civilian dress, he wore a straw hat. During the war he found his true element, and for the first time his hat took on a "twist" of character. On his return in 1919 the cocky battered hat seemed out of keeping with the rank of brigadier general—MacArthur didn't feel that way but everybody else did! But how do you tell a young general, the Army's youngest division commander, just home from the wars with thirteen decorations, including the Croix de Guerre, Distinguished Service Cross, and Distinguished Service Medal, that his hat is just not right—Army, that is?

General Peyton C. March, Chief of Staff before General Pershing, had a job for young MacArthur which was going to put a lot of stiffness in his backbone—and incidentally into his floppy, bedraggled hat. March told him to take over West Point.

He took command on June 12, 1919, and arrived at the Academy wearing the famous hat. Indeed there is a painting at the Academy by Arthur Dawson showing the General impeccably attired, but his hat looks in a deplorable state of disrepair. General Robert M. (John) Danford, who was commandant of the Academy under MacArthur, tells the ending of the story regarding his famous World War I cap. Major General Charles F. Thompson, also on the staff (he was only a major then), a close friend of MacArthur, finally said this to the General: "My God, MacArthur, that hat—you'll simply have to buy a new one, remember you are the superintendent of West Point." Reluctantly and probably a little nostalgically MacArthur bought a new hat.

MacArthur bought something else—a new lease on life for West Point. Some 3,445 graduates had seen service in the war. Their training had been a very hurried affair. West Point became an officers' training school rather than a military academy. At the war's end the young officers who had been commissioned without finishing the full four-year term had to return to West Point. This caused an extraordinary situation. One half of the cadets had officers' bars, the others were still cadets. Something of the spirit of West Point was gone, for the whole corps was split within itself. Furthermore, the famous West Point honor system had gone with the spirit. The situation was chaotic, and many young men who had planned on making the Army their career resigned rather than continue under those conditions. The honor system caused the most worry. Said the Secretary of War:

"Men may be inexact, or even untruthful, in ordinary matters, and suffer as consequence only the disteem of their associates, or the inconveniences of unfavorable litigation, but the inexact and untruthful soldier trifles with the lives of his fellow men and the honor of his government; and it is therefore no matter of idle pride, but rather of stern disciplinary necessity, that makes West Point require of her students a character of trustworthiness which knows no evasions."

It was into this situation that MacArthur was thrown: to save West Point. He came armed with a War Department directive to overcome some of the obstacles which had kept the Academy in a state of turmoil for nearly three years and which now, with the returning West

Point veterans, threatened to hinder the new crop of young students who intended to make the Army their career. One of these plans was to reduce the usual four-year course to three years. This failed.

MacArthur saw a lot more in his new post than eradicating the wartime difficulties. He had learned much during World War I and was determined to liberalize West Point as much as possible. He also saw something else: "My assumption of the command of the United States Military Academy synchronized with the ending of an epoch in the life of this institution. With the termination of the world war the mission of West Point at once became the preparation of officer personnel for the next possible future war. . . ."

He saw that there must be a new relationship between the officers of the future army and the men; above all he realized that the Army had to think differently, act differently, and train differently. Later, as Chief of Staff, he was to appeal to Congress along these lines. West Point, too, was his training ground for the battles that were to come in the soldier-politician arena of Washington. ("I am a soldier, not a political engineer," he said when somebody suggested to him that one day he would become Chief of Staff.)

The new West Point officer, he said, would be required in future to be a "type possessing all of the cardinal military virtues as of yore but possessing an intimate understanding of the mechanics of human nature, a comprehensive grasp of world and national affairs, and a liberalization of concept which amounts to a change in psychology of command."

MacArthur saw all this, but he was living in an era that wanted nothing to do with anything military. West Point was the last thing Washington wanted to hear about; so, for that matter, was the Army. The war was over—let's forget it. Everybody crawled back into their holes, pulled the warm, cozy blanket of a short-lived prosperity over their heads.

What MacArthur's aims were can best be described in the code he wrote for the Academy: "To hold fast to those policies typified in the motto of the Academy—DUTY, HONOR, COUNTRY, to cling to thoroughness as to a lode star, to continue to inculcate the habit of industry, to implant as of old the gospel of cleanliness—to be clean, to live clean, and to think clean—and yet to introduce a new atmosphere of liberalization in doing away with provincialism, a substitution of subjective for objective discipline, a progressive increase of cadet responsibility tending to develop initiative and force of character rather than automatic performance of stereotyped functions, to broaden the curriculum so as to be abreast of the best modern thought on education, to bring West Point into a new and closer relationship with the Army at large. . . ."

When the "honor system" began to show cracks in its structure prior to MacArthur's superintendentship an old system set up by the Academy's first superintendent, Colonel Sylvanus Thayer, had been reintroduced. An offender had to write out the reasons for his offense, and it would appear the following morning on the commandant's desk. Danford tells also how he suggested to MacArthur that the tactical officers in each barracks could hear the reasons across their desks just as simply. Furthermore, it would save quite a lot of work and time. "Good," said MacArthur; "put it into effect right away."

MacArthur in like manner streamlined the activities of the Academy and laid great emphasis on athletics. On

the gymnasium is this plaque bearing the words of Mac-
Arthur:

> Upon the fields of friendly strife,
> Are sown the seed that,
> Upon other fields on other days,
> Will bear the fruits of victory.

The General meant it too. He made physical training
and intramural sports compulsory. And while always a
strict disciplinarian he could close his eyes to the ex-
uberance of a victory over another competitor—for example, the Navy. Once, after a particularly glorious win,
the cadets held a "shirttail parade" after lights out. They
marched around the parade ground singing at the top of
their voices, then collected piles of firewood and built a
bonfire. The officer in charge tumbled out of his bed to
investigate the racket, realized what it was all about, and
discreetly went back to bed. The following morning,
however, Commandant General Danford wondered
what Superintendent General MacArthur would say.

MacArthur rang for his commandant first thing the
following morning.

MacArthur: "Quite a racket last night, wasn't
there?"

Danford: "There certainly was, General."

MacArthur: "How many 'skins' did you turn in?"

Danford drew a long breath. "None, sir."

MacArthur stood up and struck the desk. "Good! I
nearly got up and joined them myself."

MacArthur always displayed a good sense of humor
at West Point and knew when to close an eye to the be-
havior of his charges. Even as a senior classman during
his student years he had shown this quality. Once, as
officer of the day, he caught several young plebes, who

had left a formal West Point dance, playing poker in the locker room. MacArthur said: "Gentlemen, one look at the gathering convinces me that you have in hand matters more serious than the promenade you have just left. However, if I were you, I would refrain from studying military tactics after classes and enjoy the romantic recreation prepared for you."

MacArthur then saluted and left the room. The incident was not reported. Now, as superintendent, the General hadn't changed.

He revitalized the Academy; he fought for it in Washington; he gave it back its spirit. Indeed few people realize that the modern army of World War II was the direct outgrowth of what he foresaw would take place in the next world conflict. In 1921, in his report to the War Department, he said that the Academy was faced with "certain new demands . . . to prepare for any possible future war . . . to deliver a product trained with a view to teaching, leading, and inspiring the modern citizen to become an effective officer or soldier."

MacArthur for the next fifteen years was to harp along these same lines. He was to be called "warmonger," "sensationalist." Even when he was at West Point he was denied funds for broadening the educational base of the Academy. Yet MacArthur somehow modernized West Point. On what limited funds he had he brought in top teachers; he brought courses such as the scientific classes of aerodynamics, chemistry, and electricity up to date; he introduced new courses in economics, government, special studies on Europe and the Far East. True he was a strict disciplinarian, but anybody who studied while he was there—and since—received a military education second to none.

General MacArthur was married from West Point in

1922. To each one of the 1,700 cadets the couple sent a small white monogrammed box tied with red, white, and blue ribbon, containing a piece of wedding cake. Each cadet also received an "at-home card," and he was invited to meet the new Mrs. MacArthur in groups of fifty.

Two months later General MacArthur and his bride were on their way to the Philippines. MacArthur could not know it then, but the islands were to be his future. He was commanded to take over the 23rd Infantry Brigade and the Philippine Division, stationed at Manila; furthermore, he was charged with strengthening the islands' defenses. He was to remain there for two years, on this tour of duty. But as he and his new wife left for the Far East, MacArthur knew he was leaving behind a modernized military academy, a West Point that would only too soon be called upon to produce new leaders for a second world conflict and again—in 1950.

6. Chief of Staff

As Hitler increased his strength in Germany in the years 1931 through 1935—the very next year his troops goose-stepped into the Rhineland in violation of the Versailles Treaty with orders to goose-step right out again if the French or anyone else objected or resisted —the United States Government was steadily whittling down its appropriations for national defense.

It was not Douglas MacArthur's fault. He was Chief of Staff in those critical years of the rise of Naziism. He fought many a verbal duel with Congress for more money, which would have meant more men, more equipment, more airplanes—more of everything needed to get ready for war—but he got less and less money for running the Army, and he wound up an unprecedented five-year tour as Chief of Staff embittered with the taunts and cries of his critics ringing in his ears.

Those were the years when the post-1929 depression was taking an awful bite out of the American economy. Further, those in and out of Congress who thought that Hitler and Mussolini were stuffed mountebanks who posed no threat to our security and that the peace of Versailles would endure were not inclined to put American boys into uniform.

General MacArthur at fifty was the youngest Chief of

Staff in American history when he took over the post in
October 1930. He had just completed a two-year tour
of duty as commander of the Philippines Department—
his father had held the same post twenty-eight years before—and was commander of the 9th Army Corps Area
in San Francisco at the time of the appointment. Between the years 1922 and 1930 he had spent four years
in the Philippines and four years at army establishments
in the United States. He made one official trip outside
the country during this later period, when he headed the
American Olympic Team to Holland, prior to his de-
parture for the second time to the Philippines, in 1928.

Those who did not like MacArthur said he became
Chief of Staff through "pull." They claimed that his
wife's family influenced President Hoover's choice of
MacArthur for the top army job. But it was a good year
after their amicable Reno divorce in 1929 that Mac-
Arthur took over as Chief of Staff.

Douglas MacArthur inherited an army that was at a
peacetime low. In one of his memorable reports as Chief
of Staff—that for the fiscal year ending June 30, 1932—
he recalled that the National Defense Act of 1920,
which was the basis of our supposed military posture—
had provided that our Regular Army should comprise
approximately 18,000 officers and 280,000 men.

"During the decade just past this strength has, in the
interests of immediate economy, been progressively reduced, until appropriations are now made on the basis
of 12,000 officers and 125,250 men, including the
Philippine Scout contingent. On June 30, 1932, the
actual figures were 12,180 officers and 119,888 enlisted
men. This is below the point of safety."

MacArthur tossed out some interesting comparisons.
Of the six world powers in 1930—ourselves, Britain,

France, Italy, Japan, and Russia—the United States had the lowest number of active soldiers (including the air force) per 1,000 population. The figure was 1.06. Russia had 3.95. Britain had 5.10. France and Italy had 9.50 and 9.47 respectively. Japan had 3.57.

MacArthur also presented a table showing that as the wealthiest nation in the world we nevertheless maintained the lowest number of soldiers per billion dollars of national wealth. He showed that each of sixteen other nations—we were the wealthiest and fourth in world population—maintained a military establishment exceeding in strength the aggregate of our Regular Army, National Guard, and Organized Reserves. In our overseas garrisons (every one of which was to prove vital in World War II) we maintained about 1,915 officers and 36,080 men. These were posted at Hawaii, Panama, Puerto Rico, the Philippines, China, and Alaska.

Deducting various "overheads" in officers and men required for military schools, the War Department, rivers and harbors, et cetera, MacArthur found that for tactical purposes—namely, defense of the Continental United States—we had just 3,000 officers and 55,000 men. These were scattered through the country. It was doubtful whether we could have put into the field in an emergency even a small, well-balanced force.

And yet Congress was seriously considering a 2,000-man cut in total officer strength. MacArthur went to the extreme of trying to comb out some of the chair-borne captains, majors, and colonels who were holding down desk jobs in Washington and could have been used in the field.

MacArthur, pacing his office next to the White House and chain-smoking through a ten-inch carved oriental cigarette holder, said:

"I have humiliated myself. . . . I have almost licked the boots of some gentlemen to get funds for the motorization and mechanization of the Army. Unless we move quickly we will be a beaten nation, paying huge indemnities after the next war. The Army is below the danger line."

It remained that way until Pearl Harbor. It was again in that condition at the time of Korea.

For his troubles MacArthur was called a warmonger by none other than the late Senator Gerald P. Nye, who was to become one of the outstanding isolationists of our time and a leader of the "America First" movement that believed we could stick our heads in the sand and refuse to discharge our responsibilities as a world power —much less protect ourselves.

Others called MacArthur a "polished popinjay," a "bellicose swashbuckler." If MacArthur lost his temper, he did so privately. Pleading with congressional committees for funds, he was always polite but firm.

And as he fought to build our defenses, MacArthur as Chief of Staff did a tremendous amount of reorganization and modernization work in the Army that existed at that time.

To the Distinguished Service Medal he already possessed there was added an Oak Leaf Cluster for this performance:

"As Chief of Staff of the Army of the United States since October 21, 1930, he has performed his many important and exacting duties with signal success. He devised and developed the Four-Army organization of our land forces; he conceived and established the General Headquarters Air Force, thus immeasurably increasing the effectiveness of our air defenses; he initiated a comprehensive program of modernization in the

Army's tactics, equipment, training, and organization.

"In addition, the professional counsel and assistance he has continuously rendered to the President, to the Secretary of War, and to the Congress have been distinguished by such logic, vision, and accuracy as to contribute markedly to the formulation of sound defense policies and the enactment of progressive laws for promoting the nation's security."

Under his stewardship the Army woke up to tank warfare and to mechanization in general. MacArthur espoused the Christie tank (developed by J. Walter Christie, of Linden, New Jersey, but sold to Russia and other countries because of congressional niggardliness on appropriations). MacArthur managed in his first year as Chief of Staff to get seven such tanks for testing. He also sponsored the testing of the semi-automatic Garand rifle with which our soldiers were equipped in World War II.

In his report of 1931 MacArthur related that the Army had discarded the idea that within it a separate mechanized force should be organized as to contain within itself the power of carrying on a complete action, from first contact to final victory. The theory that MacArthur supported vigorously was this:

". . . that each of the older arms should utilize any types of these vehicles as will enable it better and more surely to carry out the particular combat tasks it has been traditionally assigned. Under this system mechanization would permeate the whole Army, but it would be applied by each arm only as an additional means of securing victory."

Scorning the idea of a mechanized elite corps, MacArthur broke up at Fort Eustis the independent "mechanized force" and made these assignments: the cavalry would develop combat vehicles to enhance its power in reconnaissance, counter-reconnaissance, flank action, pursuit, et cetera. One of the cavalry regiments would be exclusively so equipped. The infantry would give attention to machines tending to increase its striking power against strong enemy positions.

"Every part of the Army," MacArthur reported, "will adopt mechanization—and motorization—as far as it is practicable and desirable. To the greatest extent possible machines will be used to increase the mobility, security, and striking power of every ground arm, but no separate corps will be established in the vain hope that through a utilization of machines it can absorb the missions, and duplicate the capabilities, of all others."

In the same report, 1931, MacArthur laid down the fundamentals of a general mobilization plan. In its elements, the plan was the same with which we went to war in 1941. It set forth the Selective Service System with its classifications and deferments; it set forth Army procurement programs that would be dovetailed with those of the Navy to avoid waste and competitive bidding among the services; it provided for allocation of plants, for commodity committees to acquire the strategic matériel of war; it urged institution of price controls in the event of war; it planned for control of priorities in material; it advocated a labor administration to bring worker and job together and to keep them together.

MacArthur clearly understood, as had Bernard Baruch in World War I (and later in World War II, now in the Korean war) the necessity for mobilization of all our resources. Time and again the General emphasized the responsibility of each citizen, under our Constitution, for bearing arms in defense of our liberties. If a man could not bear arms, MacArthur held, at least he could do his share in other directions.

One of MacArthur's great achievements as Chief of Staff was to put into effect the four-army system for insuring the prompt and unified employment in an emergency of existing elements of the Army of the United States. For strategic purposes, the country was divided into four army areas and for administrative purposes into nine corps areas. The four army areas were natural defensive regions: the first area was the eastern seaboard; the second was the Great Lakes region; the third was the southwest; the fourth was the Far West and the west central states.

Under this scheme every existing unit was assigned to a definite place in a larger tactical organization and each was provided with a commander and his staff. All echelons, from lowest to highest, were so organized, and there was a complete chain of command right up to the Commander in Chief at the White House.

In the event of trouble, the four-army plan was designed to provide trained officers and trained combat units—whether for overseas service or for defense of well-studied domestic areas.

MacArthur fought for efficiency against continuing budget cuts. In 1932 the Army got $335,000,000 from Congress. In 1933 Congress lopped $50,000,000 off this. In 1934 it cut another $16,000,000 out. Within two years the Regular Army budget was slashed by 38 per cent.

MacArthur again warned that adherence to the doctrine that "a million men would spring to arms overnight" had cost us fearful prices several times.

In the realm of mechanization MacArthur laid the

groundwork for the development of Fort Knox, Kentucky, as the headquarters of armored forces.

Possibly his greatest achievement was the establishment of a general headquarters air force, the first concentration of fighter and bomber planes within the United States. As he envisaged the planes of this force, "they are to be used just as you would use a slingshot. They are to be thrown at the point where they will be the most damaging. For cohesion, co-ordination, and to prevent their dissipation on minor missions, they are held together as a great general reserve under the commanding general in the field.

"Their uses would be varied. They could be used as a great deciding factor in a mass combat. They could be used for rapid reinforcement at distant threatened points, such as our outposts in Panama or in Hawaii. They could be used in independent missions of destruction, aimed at the vital arteries of a nation, or they might, of necessity, be divided up and used in detail."

As a minimum striking force MacArthur wanted 1,000 planes divided into five wings.

There was only one time, according to the *West Pointer,* when "Doug ever took his finger off his number." That was in the summer of 1932, when it befell him as Chief of Staff to head the troops that routed, under higher orders, the ragged, half-starved army of bonus marchers from the national capital.

For two months, almost in the shadow of our magnificent Capitol, the bonus army—with some Communist inspiration—lived in the hope of persuading Congress to pay out immediately nearly $2,500,000,000 outstanding in the veterans' adjusted service certificates of World War I.

The first marchers, about three hundred men from western states, reached Washington on May 30, 1932. They lived in half-wrecked buildings on Pennsylvania Avenue. MacArthur suspected that men from his old Rainbow Division of World War I might be among the needy; characteristically, he ordered mobile kitchens out to feed the men. New arrivals came throughout June. They camped in vacant lots; they brought their wives and children, installing them in wretched shacks made from packing crates and odds and ends of lumber. Campfires at night threw weird, flickering lights against the sky. The wiseacres dubbed the shanty town "Hooverville" in derision of a President who endured a depression not of his making.

Brigadier General Pelham D. Glassford (retired) was chief of Washington's city police force. He had a difficult time as the bonus army grew. Rumors of a "raid" on the White House kitchens compelled the police to lock the iron gates to the grounds. The marchers put the heat on members of Congress; the usual blazing sun of Washington did its best to keep tempers high.

On July 24 a rag, tag, and bobtail mob of vets began to march toward the White House, through the capital's business district. Police and detectives tried to break them up. At the Treasury, adjoining the White House grounds, a brief scuffle grew into a melee with the police, who drove the marchers back a block. One group of veterans made an end run around to a White House gate where the sight of police ready with tear-gas guns froze them in their tracks. Mr. Hoover was at work inside; possibly he heard the taunts flung at him from the pavement.

Tension mounted in the next few days. There were new clashes with Glassford's police. Glassford's forces could not cope with the bonus army without risking bloodshed.

The worst day of all was July 28. About 200 marchers on lower Pennsylvania Avenue were joined at noon by 5,000 others who had escaped rope barriers flung up by the police. In mid-afternoon, in blistering heat, about 1,000 policemen attempted to drive the horde back from the center of the city. Wild scrimmages ensued. Defending themselves against rocks and bats, the police had to open fire; two marchers were killed and fifty were injured.

General Glassford said he could not maintain order. Accordingly the District Commissioners (who govern Washington after a fashion) asked Mr. Hoover for help.

At 3 P.M. immediate orders were issued to MacArthur by Patrick J. Hurley, then Secretary of War, who told the General that the President had heard from the District Commissioners of their inability to keep order.

"You will have United States troops proceed immediately to the scene of disorder," said Hurley. "Co-operate fully with the District of Columbia police force which is now in charge. Surround the affected area and clear it without delay.

"Turn over all prisoners to the civil authorities.

"In your orders, insist that any women and children who may be in the affected area be accorded every consideration and kindness. Use all humanity consistent with the due execution of this order."

MacArthur wasted no time. From Fort Meade, Maryland, he ordered five small tanks put on trucks and deployed with mounted cavalrymen to the White House area. Discarding a white summer suit, he put on a bemedaled uniform. He placed Brigadier General Perry L. Miles in charge of a total of about 700 infantrymen and cavalrymen. Miles told the cavalry to "demonstrate" down Pennsylvania Avenue, with the infantry skirmishing along to the rear. The avenue, between Third and Fourth streets, was to be surrounded and all bonus marchers there evicted from the area.

In late afternoon MacArthur mounted a white horse and led the troops down Pennsylvania Avenue. Someone heaved a rock at him. He turned, ordered bayonets out. The soldiers advanced toward the battered old buildings that still housed some marchers. Protected by gas masks, the troops lobbed tear-gas shells into the gaping structures. Wind blew some of the gas into the mob of 10,000 spectators who had gathered. There was a wild stampede.

Next the Army burned the old buildings and moved on to other areas of the city where the bonus marchers were camping. One by one the areas were cleared, the shacks burned. MacArthur called a halt for supper; he fed not only his own troops but the poor marchers.

Late that night MacArthur and his men arrived at Anacostia Flats, along the Potomac River, site of the largest bonus-army camp. The pitiful "army" asked for half an hour to clear out. MacArthur gave them an hour. And he gave gasoline and oil to those who had battered old cars, so that they might drive out of the city toward their homes. Then he had the camp burned.

MacArthur was violently condemned in the next few months as a brute and a bully. He remained silent. He had carried out his orders.

President Hoover gave MacArthur the job of Chief of Staff because he was the best man for it. Nor would Franklin D. Roosevelt let MacArthur go. Normally the Chief of Staff serves four years. Through Secretary of

War Dern's insistence and Roosevelt's own liking for the General, MacArthur remained an extra year. At last, in the winter of 1935, MacArthur relinquished the post to take up the appointment as military adviser **to** the Philippine Commonwealth.

7. MacArthur in the Philippines

The daredevil general of World War I was gone, so was the good-humored general who rebuilt the spirit of West Point; what was left was a lonely, embittered man who at fifty-five had apparently reached the end of his career. Let future biographers of MacArthur note one important factor when writing of the General: the worst thing that can happen to an army man is to be promoted over the heads of senior officers, for this was precisely what happened to General MacArthur, and accounts greatly for the enmity and indeed hatred he has borne all his life. He was given the superintendency of West Point as a young brigadier; he became Chief of Staff at only fifty. Furthermore, his farsightedness was ridiculed by some senior officers who felt that they had been passed over by this "popinjay," as some of his enemies politely called him in the brittle superficiality of Washington society. Whatever MacArthur's attitude today is toward Washington one can safely assume that it is greatly colored by his experience as Chief of Staff. Is it any wonder that MacArthur sometimes appears to disregard Washington? Is it any wonder that he has not returned to the place of his greatest defeat since 1937? MacArthur, history now proves, was one of America's greatest Chiefs of Staff, yet it was a bitter disappointment to him, for he was not able fully to awaken the country to his warning that "a score of nations will soon be ready for the sack of the United States." Roosevelt believed in MacArthur and remained one of his closest friends.

However, F.D.R. had a problem about the placing of MacArthur. He was still too young to let go. Roosevelt is quoted as having told a Washington official: "I must always find a way to keep Douglas close to me. If we ever have another A.E.F., he's the man to take over." Thus it was that as MacArthur's last year—an extra year; he should have relinquished his term of office midnight November 20, 1934—came to a close Roosevelt listened attentively to a plea from Manuel Quezon, first President of the Philippines. "Loan me MacArthur as military adviser to the Philippines," was what he asked.

Now, under a special section of the National Defense Act, the President is authorized to detail special officers to help certain foreign governments which the President considers friendly; furthermore, he can, if he so desires, loan troops, air, and naval units. After consultations between Roosevelt, Secretary of War George H. Dern, and President Quezon, the matter was settled. Then the plan was presented to MacArthur. According to one account it took MacArthur less than five minutes to agree. Said his critics when they heard the news: "Now he's going to be a little Napoleon in the islands." That "Napoleon" was to save many of their skins in the Pacific six years later.

MacArthur was relieved of his post as Chief of Staff on October 2, 1935, and ordered forthwith to the Philippines. Under the agreement he was to receive his regular salary (base pay about $8,000), and the Philippines, if they so wished, could pay him an additional

allowance. Quezon's government agreed to pay Mac-
Arthur an amount which has been variously stated as
being somewhere between $18,000 and $30,000. His
critics, of course, put this figure up to $50,000, saying,
"He knows which side his bread is buttered on." Mac-
Arthur is supposed to have said when he heard these
jealous rumblings, "I would not sell my sword."

Furthermore, the Philippine Government agreed to
furnish quarters for MacArthur and his staff. Mac-
Arthur was installed in a six-room, air-conditioned penthouse apartment on top of the new sumptuous Manila
Hotel.

While the MacArthurs have always been close to the
Philippines, many felt that Douglas MacArthur wanted
to retire when he finished his tenure of office as Chief
of Staff. He had gone on record on several occasions
with statements which seemed to indicate that he would
be glad to sit back and follow "cultural pursuits." One
of these was writing, and a careful study of his reports
as Chief of Staff—which his critics snidely say were
written in the first place by General Eisenhower, who
was then attached to the office of Chief of Staff—his
writings at West Point, his later communiqués all point
to his having a very definite if somewhat high-flown[1]
command of words. However, his new appointment excited him, for he was convinced even then that Japanese
aggression would not stop with China.

President Quezon promised MacArthur that the
Philippine Government would appropriate $10,000,000
per year for the new Philippine army and defense plan
which was to be put into effect. MacArthur developed a
ten-year plan, which called for speedy PT-boat type
naval units, a fast, maneuverable, compact air force, a

[1]See Appendix.

regular army of 400,000 (which included a selective-service plan calling 40,000 men per year), and defense works and fortifications throughout the islands. Mac-Arthur's plan sounded good, even though Secretary of War Stimson later called it too "optimistic."

The lights burned often and late in the air-conditioned penthouse apartment. The General, as was his habit, did a lot of his thinking and planning while pacing up and down through his long book-lined living room. His only relaxation was an occasional trip to a movie; an occasional drink: 60 per cent orange juice, 40 per cent gin. He rarely entered into Manila's social life, but occasionally warmly entertained a few guests. Sometimes, so the story goes, a guest on the floor below at the hotel would hear the General's pacing at 2 A.M. and would call the desk clerk to complain: "Doesn't that guy know what time it is?"

MacArthur knew what time it was, but the Philippine Government didn't. For one thing, President Quezon had difficulty in persuading his government to make the appropriations he had promised MacArthur. "In ten years from now," MacArthur told him, "even I would not command an invasion force to capture these islands." But the Philippine Government year after year whittled down the annual defense allotment. There were complaints about MacArthur's salary, his free living quarters. And while the Filipinos had the greatest respect for MacArthur, the Moros in particular refused to register for army duty. Not only did he have to contend with defeatism among the islanders, but he was fair game for Filipino politicians who did not like the inroads that military expenditures made into their favorite pork-barrel projects. The Japanese, too, did what they could to try to get Quezon to send home that "arrogant MacArthur."

In 1936 he was made a field marshal by the Philippine Republic. Immediately there was an outcry from his critics back in the States. Should an American general accept a rank higher than his own country has to offer, they asked? In accepting the gold baton from President Quezon, MacArthur was placed in quite an embarrassing position. If he had refused the baton, he would have hurt the pride of the Philippine people; in accepting it, he left himself wide open for attacks by his critics. But MacArthur had grown used to the bitterness, jealousy, and intrigue which seemed to dog his every step; he accepted it.

In 1937 he retired from the Army with this accolade from President Roosevelt: "Your history in war and peace is a brilliant chapter in American history." And there are some who say that Roosevelt asked him to remain on. But MacArthur was tired. He had married his second wife in 1937 and was at last domestically happy. He spent his days feverishly working to build Philippine defenses, for even he knew that he could not, by any means, complete his entire plan now that the Philippine Government had reduced the appropriations.

Manila society spoke of MacArthur as being "washed up." His failure to mingle with people was, whether the General knew it or not, one of the reasons for this. However, this was nothing new in MacArthur's make-up, he had always been somewhat of a recluse.

Even in Manila also his warnings about the Japanese were not looked upon seriously. But with Munich the tune changed sharply both in the islands and in Washington. And again when war broke out in Europe in 1939. In the Philippines the real writing on the wall appeared when the Japanese occupied northern Indo-China and signed the tripartite agreement with Italy and Germany in 1940. Yet that year the Philippine Government cut the defense appropriation to only $1,000,000 despite MacArthur's warnings, his pleading for more funds. It is said that MacArthur wanted to quit and return to the United States because of this, but he was urged by Quezon to remain and somehow finish the job. "This is a call of duty I cannot overlook," he is quoted as having said.

To his Filipino wards he exhorted: "Write your history in red on the breasts of your enemy. Only those are fit to live who are not afraid to die for their country."

By the middle of 1941 MacArthur had 20,000 Filipino regulars, 125,000 Filipino reserves, 150 Filipino pilots and a small air force, a small compact fleet of torpedo boats, and a West Point-modeled military academy.

MacArthur was sixty-one when on July 28, 1941, President Roosevelt, with the crisis mounting in the Far East, recalled him to active service as a lieutenant general and placed him in command of the United States Army forces in the Far East (USAFFE). His little Philippine army was brought into the federal service. Also in the islands and placed under MacArthur's new command were 19,000 United States Army troops and about 8,000 Army Air Force personnel equipped with about 250 planes—35 Flying Fortresses and 107 P-40 fighters among them.

The general who had been called "washed up" and dubbed the "Napoleon of the islands" had been called upon again by his country. He was there to carry the colors when on December 7 the Japanese hit Pearl Harbor.

8. "I Shall Return"

In December 1941, at the time of Pearl Harbor, the Japanese lashed out at the Philippines. First they bombed such key airfields on Luzon as Clark and Nichols, destroying many American planes which could not be dispersed in time because of lack of radar warning networks. Nor were there enough anti-aircraft guns on hand. It was one of the early instances of too little and too late.

MacArthur had 11,500 miles of Philippine coastline to defend. He could not have his troops everywhere at once and was compelled to await a Japanese invasion. It came in overwhelming numbers in northwestern Luzon on December 10 and 22, 1941. The Japanese also landed in force on the east coast of Luzon. They tossed more than 200,000 men at MacArthur's mixed defenders.

MacArthur, utilizing the classic defense of the Philippines that had been projected nearly thirty years before by General Homer Lea, avoided the pincers operation that the Japanese had hoped to pull off against him north and south of Manila. Evacuating Manila at Christmas and declaring it an open city—which was disregarded by the Japanese—he managed an orderly withdrawal into the Bataan Peninsula, jutting south into

Manila Bay and covered and protected by the island fortress of Corregidor. He sent the remainder of his bombers south from Clark Field to Mindanao, later to Australia.

The Americans threw a twenty-mile line across the neck of Bataan and contested every inch of the ground. But with a Japanese naval blockade of the islands preventing reinforcements and supplies, and with Bataan jammed by thousands of civilians who fled their homes to follow the troops, MacArthur quickly had to put the entire command on half rations.

An attempt was made to organize blockade-running from the Dutch East Indies and Australia to bring food and supplies and to smuggle in critically needed munitions by submarine. But the "friendly" people of Java, Timor, and New Guinea would not take a United States Treasury check for their efforts. They wanted cash; it had to be flown across Africa and India. The Japanese sank about fifteen blockade-runners, totaling 40,000 tons, before they ever got to Bataan. But American submarines got through, and they evacuated some personnel from the beleaguered forces.

Without decent food and medicines, the malaria-ridden, weary troops under MacArthur could do nothing but fall back southward along the Bataan Peninsula. They exacted a heavy toll of the Japanese as they did so. On half rations since mid-January of 1942, the GIs of that day went on ever smaller rations by the end of March. And they began to slaughter horses and mules to improve their diet.

It was clear to the high command in Washington that the Philippines were untenable; nothing could save them. Because of Japanese capabilities elsewhere in the Pacific, Washington decided to concentrate on building

Australia as the base from which MacArthur would
begin his long road back. Defense forces were spread
along the air and sea routes to Australia. The Hawaii
garrison was built up, as were other islands on the air
lane. A considerable force was sent to New Caledonia.
Bombers were flown via Hawaii and India to Australia.
Other aid was sent to the East Indies.

MacArthur's men fought on grimly on Bataan. They
staved off three big enemy attacks so well that Lieutenant General Masaharu Homma, a fast man with a
whisky highball and possessor of an Oxford accent, was
removed in favor of General Tomoyoki Yamashita, who
had conquered Singapore. (MacArthur later saw to it
that Yamashita was hanged at Manila for his barbarous
treatment of war prisoners and civilians.) However, it
was reported from Japanese sources that he "committed
suicide" in Manila and was cremated.

In February 1942 the War Department and President
Roosevelt ordered MacArthur to save his skill for the
long pull. He was told to proceed from Bataan and
Corregidor to Australia and assume command of the
newly designated Southwest Pacific Area. He was to
hold Australia, check the foe along the Melanesian barrier, protect land, sea, and air communications with the
Southwest Pacific, and maintain our slipping position
in the Philippines. Quite an order. Lieutenant General
Jonathan M. Wainwright, who had been conducting
field operations on Bataan, was named to succeed Mac-
Arthur as commander of the Philippine forces for their
final epic defense.

Two sixty-five-foot motor torpedo boats of the type
MacArthur had ordered for defense of the Philippines
slipped into the Corregidor dock at dusk on March 11,
1942. MacArthur, his wife, and son (in a blue zipper

jacket, khaki trousers, and khaki overseas cap), with young Arthur's Chinese amah or nurse, climbed aboard one boat. Some of the nineteen staff officers who were to go with the General to Australia boarded the other boat.

In a hidden inlet on Bataan Major General Hugh Casey, an engineer, led other MacArthur staff members aboard two more PTs. The plan was for the four boats to meet before dawn and to hide near shore for another night. But the PTs had taken a beating in the war and could not make their rated thirty-nine knots. The two groups became separated and were forced to risk a daylight voyage, not joining until about noon. They headed for Mindanao, one hundred miles to the southeast of Manila, over a choppy sea that made most of the passengers seasick. At dusk a Japanese warship was sighted on the horizon. The crews cut the PTs engines; the four lay still. But the Japanese ship had not spotted them and passed on.

Toward dawn the PTs made Mindanao. There was an agonizing three-day wait for three Flying Fortresses that had been sent north to pick up the party. Only two arrived; baggage, arms, and equipment were jettisoned. All got aboard. The planes took off about midnight, March 16, and flew for about eleven hours to northern Australia. They went near the conquered East Indies, past enemy airdromes and troop centers on New Guinea and Timor.

Fourteen of the MacArthur staff headed for Melbourne. MacArthur rested for a day. Then, from Darwin, he went by train into the desert to Birdum, 250 miles south. From there he had to drive 500 miles farther south on a new military highway through desolate land. Near Alice Springs reporters finally found him, resting in a railroad car. With the General was an old friend, Brigadier General Patrick Hurley, United States Minister to New Zealand. The reporters wanted a statement, Hurley informed MacArthur. MacArthur wrote:

"The President of the United States ordered me to break through the Japanese line and proceed from Corregidor to Australia for the purpose, as I understand it, of organizing the American offensive against Japan. A primary purpose of this is the relief of the Philippines. I came through and I shall return."

As MacArthur's train approached Melbourne on a crisp March morning (autumn in Australia), 4,000 gathered to meet him at the station. Assorted generals and admirals in khaki, and an American guard of honor, and seven brown Filipino soldiers awaited. The train stopped. There was a wait. MacArthur stepped out, in a plain, faded khaki jacket, open at the neck and without his four stars of rank, and sharply pressed khaki trousers. There was a touch of gold on his garrison cap. In his right hand swung a bamboo swagger stick.

MacArthur stepped up to a microphone.

"I have every confidence in the ultimate success of our joint cause, but success in modern war requires something more than courage and willingness to die. It requires careful preparation. . . . No general can make something from nothing. My success or failure will depend primarily upon the resources which our respective governments place at my disposal. My faith in them is complete. In any event I shall do my best. I shall keep the soldier's faith."

"What's that?" asked a scribbling Australian reporter, who couldn't catch the last word.

"I shall keep the soldier's faith," Douglas MacArthur repeated firmly into the microphone.

MacArthur was scarcely in Australia when the Japanese opened an all-out attack on Wainwright's positions on Bataan. It lasted a week, without letup. Jap artillery began to shell American field hospitals. The front lines were penetrated. Disaster stared the exhausted defenders in the face.

Wainwright radioed the War Department from Corregidor on April 9: "Shortly after the flag of truce passed through the front line this morning, hostilities ceased for the most part in Bataan. At about ten o'clock this morning General King was sent for, to confer with the Japanese commander. He has not returned, as of 7 o'clock P.M., nor has result of conference been disclosed. Since the fall of Bataan the hostile air force has renewed its attack on Corregidor. This island was heavily bombed this afternoon but has suffered no damage of military consequence."

Corregidor and its satellite island forts guarding the mouth of Manila Bay—Forts Drum and Hughes—held out for nearly a month longer, with counter-battery and anti-aircraft fire. On May 5 the Japanese, after a week of bombardment that buried some defenses under rocky landslides, came ashore on the north point of kidney-shaped Corregidor. The next day the exhausted Americans surrendered honorably.

Just before Corregidor fell Wainwright wrote this letter:

"As I write this we are subjected to terrific air and artillery bombardment, and it is unreasonable to expect that we can hold out for long. We have done our best, both here and on Bataan, and although beaten we are still unashamed."

Technically, Bataan and Corregidor were defeats for MacArthur's forces. Actually, they were skillfully conducted delaying operations against an overwhelmingly superior enemy. MacArthur, Wainwright & Co. exacted a heavy price from the Japanese. They tied up crack Japanese troops for nearly five months when they might have been employed elsewhere. They denied to the Japanese for the same period the use of Manila harbor, one of the finest in the Orient. The time gained enabled men and matériel to flow to Australia, New Caledonia, and elsewhere in the Pacific.

When he heard of Bataan's fall, MacArthur said: "No army has ever done so much with so little. Nothing became it like its last hour of trial and agony. To the weeping mothers of its dead I only say that the sacrifice and halo of Jesus of Nazareth has descended upon their sons and that God will take them to Himself."

When Corregidor fell a month later, MacArthur said: "Corregidor needs no comment from me. It has sounded its own story at the mouth of its guns. It has scrolled its own epitaph on the enemy tablets."

Winston Churchill has recorded that when he was visiting Franklin D. Roosevelt at the White House late in December 1941 and learned of the "approaching fate" of MacArthur on Bataan and Corregidor, he "thought it right" to show to Mr. Roosevelt and Henry L. Stimson, then Secretary of War, the dispatch which the British War Office had sent in the dark days of May 1940 to Viscount Gort, then commander of the sorely tried British Expeditionary Force that was falling back upon Dunkirk.

The War Office message told Gort that he would be ordered to return to England with a few officers and turn over command to a corps commander. The message said that on political grounds it would be bad for the Germans to capture Gort and it would be "a need-less triumph" for the enemy.

Churchill concedes it is possible that the tenor of this message influenced other great events and the fortunes of "another valiant commander," namely MacArthur. Churchill says Roosevelt and Stimson read the message with deep attention; Stimson asked for a copy of it. Churchill says it may have been "that this influenced them in the right decision" that was taken when Mac-Arthur was ordered some weeks later to transfer his command to Wainwright and to head for Australia, thereby avoiding death or capture. "I should like to think this was true," Churchill has written in his ad-mirable volume, *Their Finest Hour.*

Mr. Stimson in his book *On Active Service in Peace and War,* in which McGeorge Bundy was his collabo-rator, has told of the failure of attempts to run the Japanese blockade of the Philippines so that aid might reach MacArthur. Stimson emphasized that the gallant forces under MacArthur and Quezon were thus handed the task of fighting a delaying action and of maintain-ing American honor in the Philippines.

Mr. Stimson paid tribute to "the skillful and vastly courageous operations" of MacArthur's forces. As we have reported, these forces were hopelessly outnumbered and underequipped, but, as Mr. Stimson related, "they exacted losses from the enemy that left no doubt in any mind of the quality of the American soldier."

MacArthur and Quezon in those final bitter days of Bataan radioed message upon message to Washington, beseeching the help that never came—and could not have come—except for a trickle of supplies by sub-marine. They were sent only admonitions of encouragement when they wanted and needed bullets, men, food, and medicine.

Early in February of 1942 Quezon wirelessed a bomb-shell to the White House. He suggested to Roosevelt that the United States should declare the Philippines inde-pendent and that this country and Japan should then proceed to neutralize the islands. All troops would be withdrawn and the Philippine Army mustered out. Quezon threw in a few gratuitous remarks about the lack of American help.

Francis B. Sayre, son-in-law of the late President Woodrow Wilson and then High Commissioner in the Philippines, subscribed to Quezon's scheme.

It was MacArthur's lot to forward the Quezon and Sayre messages. The General tacked on this one:

"Since I have no air or sea protection you must be prepared at any time to figure on the complete destruc-tion of this command. You must determine whether the mission of delay would be better furthered by the tem-porizing plan of Quezon or by my continued battle effort. The temper of the Filipinos [and few were better judges than MacArthur] is one of almost violent resent-ment against the United States. Every one of them ex-pected help, and when it has not been forthcoming they believe they have been betrayed in favor of others."

MacArthur made it clear that he had no illusions about the future, but he wanted to know what to do.

"So far as the military angle is concerned," he added, "the problem presents itself as to whether the plan of President Quezon might offer the best possible solution of what is about to be a disastrous debacle. It would not affect the ultimate solution in the Philippines, for that would be determined by the results in other thea-ters. If the Japanese Government rejects President

Quezon's proposition it would psychologically strengthen our hold because of their Prime Minister's public statement offering independence. If it accepts it, we lose no military advantage because we would still secure at least equal delay. Please instruct me."

One can imagine the reaction in the Pentagon and at the White House. Quezon seemed to be selling out despite his public pronouncements. Sayre, and worst of all MacArthur, appeared to be backing Quezon's scheme. Stimson and the Chief of Staff, General of the Army George C. Marshall, rushed to see Roosevelt. The President asked Marshall what he proposed to do. Marshall let Stimson answer. Stimson felt that the Quezon idea played into the Japanese hands, that it would ruin the friendship between the Philippines and the United States, that Japan could not be trusted to keep any agreement about neutralizing the islands, and that the United States and Japan would be held equally guilty of destroying the Philippines.

Marshall spent the afternoon working up a reply to MacArthur; Stimson drafted one for Quezon. The upshot was this message from Roosevelt to MacArthur, dated February 9, 1942:

"In the second section of this message I am making, through you an immediate reply to President Quezon's proposals of February 8. My reply must emphatically deny the possibility of this Government's agreement to the political aspects of President Quezon's proposal. I authorize you to arrange for the capitulation of the Filipino elements of the defending forces, when and if in your opinion that course appears necessary and always having in mind that the Filipino troops are in the service of the United States. Details of all necessary arrangements will be left in your hands, including plans for segregation of forces and the withdrawal, if your judgment so dictates, of American elements to Fort Mills [Corregidor]. The timing also will be left to you.

"American forces will continue to keep our flag flying in the Philippines so long as there remains any possibility of resistance. I have made these decisions in complete understanding of your military estimate that accompanied President Quezon's message to me. The duty and the necessity of resisting Japanese aggression to the last transcends in importance any other obligation now facing us in the Philippines.

"There has been gradually welded into a common front a globe-encircling opposition to the predatory powers that are seeking the destruction of individual liberty and freedom of government. We cannot afford to have this line broken in any particular theater. As the most powerful member of this coalition we cannot display weakness in fact or in spirit anywhere. It is mandatory that there be established once and for all in the minds of all peoples complete evidence that the American determination and indomitable will to win carries on down to the last unit.

"I therefore give you this most difficult mission in full understanding of the desperate situation to which you may be shortly reduced. The service that you and the American members of your command can render to your country in the titanic struggle now developing is beyond all possibility of appraisement. I particularly request that you proceed rapidly to the organization of your forces and your defenses so as to make your resistance as effective as circumstances will permit and as prolonged as humanly possible.

"If the evacuation of President Quezon and his cabinet appears reasonably safe they would be honored and greatly welcomed in the United States. They should come here via Australia. This applies also to the High Commissioner. Mrs. Sayre and your family should be given this opportunity if you consider it advisable. You yourself, however, must determine action to be taken in view of circumstances."

Roosevelt asked MacArthur to radio the gist of his plans in accordance with the above instructions. He also asked the General to pass along to Quezon the second section of the message. This part, in effect, told Quezon that the United States was pledged to give the Philippines their independence in 1946, that Japanese offers or promises could never be relied upon, that whatever happened to MacArthur's garrison, the American forces would return "and drive the last remnant of the invaders from your soil."

MacArthur himself could not have written it better. Quezon, with this shot in the arm, promised to abide by Roosevelt's message. MacArthur characteristically said he would fight on to the end, and that in no circumstances would he surrender the Filipino troops under him.

Characteristically, too, MacArthur said he would keep his family at his side; Quezon could not leave because of his health but was later persuaded to go, and reached Australia before MacArthur. He has since died of tuberculosis.

In his book Stimson remarks that MacArthur and Quezon had demonstrated their skill and courage, yet "neither appeared to appreciate the moral abdication involved in the proposal of a neutralized Philippines."

Whatever Quezon felt MacArthur appreciated everything only too well; it must have been easy in the air-conditioned purlieus of Washington in 1942 to have flashed hortatory messages to Bataan, where the temperature under an implacable sun and before a tenacious, skillful foe was in the hundreds and Americans were dying like flies. In those days—even as today—Washington and the rest of the United States were only partially mobilized; there was a groping, fumbling understanding of what war meant (the men on Bataan knew); even as today there was the desire to carry on "business as usual" and not to do anything too drastic on the home front that might boomerang politically.

9. The Long Road Back

"Rally to me. Let the indomitable spirit of Bataan and Corregidor lead on. . . . For the land of your sacred birth, strike!

"Let no heart be faint. Let every arm be steeled. The guidance of Divine God points to the way. Follow in His name to the Holy Grail of righteous victory."

These were the words of Douglas MacArthur as he stepped ashore through the surf onto sun-bathed Leyte, on October 20, 1944.

It was his destiny to liberate the Philippines. He had promised to come back, and he did. As the cruiser *Nashville* neared shore in Leyte Gulf, MacArthur ate a hearty breakfast, went briefly on deck, and puffed the corncob pipe. He went below and napped for an hour. He was up at 10 A.M., watched the preliminary bombardment, heard that the troops were half a mile inland on schedule. He had an early lunch in his cabin.

A landing craft took MacArthur ashore soon afterward. He waded the last few feet. "Believe it or not, we're here," he said. "I will stay," he added, "for the duration."

In sixteen months MacArthur and his forces had come back 2,500 miles north from Milne Bay, New

Guinea, whence his counter-offensive against the Japanese had started.

From his many months in Australia MacArthur had watched the islands closely, receiving intelligence reports from guerrillas and from American agents who were put ashore on various islands by submarine and were equipped with shortwave radios so that they might send coded messages on Japanese ship and troop movements among the archipelago.

He had planned to re-enter the Philippines in December 1944. The assault would have been aimed at the southernmost main island of Mindanao. The Japanese were in strength there; it would have been a battle, particularly around the city of Davao in the south.

The Navy, under Admiral Nimitz's over-all direction, was busy with carrier strikes softening up Japanese defenses, taking pictures, feeling out the enemy. In the early fall of 1944 a naval aviator was shot down over Leyte; he got ashore unhurt and was concealed by friendly Filipinos. He was picked up not long after and made a startling intelligence report which led to alteration of the plan for reconquering the Philippines. He reported that Leyte, rather than Mindanao, would be a comparative pushover. Further, it had good beaches.

The report was confirmed by photographs. MacArthur and the Chiefs of Staff in Washington hastily revised their plans. Only a few months before MacArthur had gone to Hawaii to meet President Roosevelt and to win with his persuasiveness a powerful argument against the Navy. The Navy wanted to skip the Philippines, hit Formosa, and prepare for a landing on the China coast. MacArthur said no; he pointed out our moral obligation to retake the Philippines, convinced Roosevelt it could be done without the blood baths that the Navy and the Marines had suffered in their Central Pacific operations against such Jap strongholds as Tarawa, Eniwetok, and Saipan.

The report on Jap weakness at Leyte speeded up the reconquest of the islands by three months. Our troops sailed in gigantic convoys from Manus, in the Admiralty Islands, and Hollandia, in Dutch New Guinea. It was the mightiest armada yet seen in the Pacific.

One can imagine MacArthur's emotion on stepping ashore. From Australia he had seen the enemy pushing right into the Coral Sea, the high-water mark of their advance south. In mid-1942 the Japanese had landed at Gona on the northeast coast of New Guinea and were pushing inland toward the Owen Stanley range of mountains; they would have reached Port Moresby. Australian troops were rushed by air and turned them back. American and Australian ground troops routed the Japs in the Buna section of New Guinea that fall and winter. New American divisions arriving from home turned the tide.

The Japanese tried a small flanking movement at Milne Bay on the eastern nose of New Guinea in late August 1942. Americans and Australians were waiting for them. It was the start of the long road back.

Apart from MacArthur's command, American forces in the South Pacific were busy. Marines went into Guadalcanal some 1,200 miles northeast of Australia, blocking, in effect, any enemy drive for New Zealand.

In 1943 the Japanese were stopped in their tracks as they tried, with an enormous convoy, to reinforce Lae, New Guinea; in the battle of the Bismarck Sea in March of that year an entire convoy of twenty-two transports and warships was destroyed.

In mid-1943 MacArthur's forces were definitely mov-

ing back northward. He had command by that time of
the South Pacific theater; troops went into New Georgia
and along the New Guinea coast to Nassau Bay. The
Americans wound up the year by landing in force on
western New Britain. With their footing on Bougain-
ville, the Allied forces had neutralized the great Jap
base at Rabaul, in eastern New Britain.

MacArthur leapfrogged rapidly along the New
Guinea coast in 1944—to Saidor, then to the Admiralty Islands, to Hollandia. From there MacArthur, always seizing air bases in advance to protect his next
moves, went to Noemfoor, Biak, Sansapor, Morotai—
all forgotten names now but about 600 miles from
Leyte.

The Leyte campaign was tough to the end; it is history. It broke the back of Japanese resistance in the
islands. Our victory gave us air bases from which to
hammer enemy air strength on Luzon. MacArthur's
forces, aided by the 7th Fleet, went into Luzon—as the
Japanese had in 1941—by way of Lingayen Gulf. They
were in Manila in February 1945.

On March 2 Douglas MacArthur set foot once again
on battle-scarred Corregidor. He saw the Stars and
Stripes hoisted on the battered white flagpole from
which the enemy had ripped it three years before. He
said: "I see the old flagstaff still stands. Haul the colors
to its peak and let no enemy ever haul them down."

He surveyed the reeking wreckage of the island,
peered into the dank tunnels under Malinta Hill in the
center of the island, and remarked, "Well, gentlemen,
it's been a long way back."

He spotted a dead Jap outside one of the tunnels.
"That," he said, "is the way I like to see them."

In Manila MacArthur found his pre-war Rolls-Royce,

unscratched, highly polished, in good condition. He also met up with his old Negro barber from Corregidor, seventy-one-year-old John M. Howell, who had trimmed the heads of Americans on that island since 1899 and had been captured and interned by the Japanese. MacArthur recognized him in an army hospital for prisoners of war. "You look me up in Manila and I'll make you the official barber," said MacArthur, pumping Howell's hand. "You've got ten more years of barbering ahead of you and then at least twenty-five years to loaf."

In the ruins of his old penthouse atop the Manila Hotel MacArthur found a charred grand piano, a ruined library, chips of his china service, burned flakes of the scrapbooks he had kept on his father and himself. There was no sign of the family silverware. A few pieces of it, nabbed by a hastily departing Jap general, were discovered a few weeks later in the cellar of a house in northeastern Manila.

10. Japan, the Springboard

In late August of 1945 Douglas MacArthur and the loyal band of men who had been "The Battling Bastards of Bataan" dropped onto Atsugi airdrome, thirty miles west of Tokyo. From the dank tunnels of Corregidor, by PT-boat and by air, road, and train down to Australia, then by leapfrogging tactics back along New Guinea and up through the Philippines—it had been a long, hard road back.

There was no blood lust among the Americans, but MacArthur had already had one bit of revenge. During negotiations for the surrender of Japan in the last fretful days of August the Japanese stalled day after day before sending their envoys to Manila to receive MacArthur's orders and to communicate the information he desired of them. They wanted more time to get their envoys ready. They wanted MacArthur's orders spelled out. Finally MacArthur wirelessed to Tokyo: "The directive from this headquarters is clear and explicit and is to be complied with without further delay."

Led by the gray-haired, round-headed vice chief of the now doomed but once arrogant Japanese General Staff, Lieutenant General Torashiro Kawabe, sixteen Japanese took off from Japan, bound for Manila, via

Le Shima. By MacArthur's orders their plane had to use "Bataan" as its radio call.

The Japanese never got to see MacArthur in Manila. They saw his chief of staff, Lieutenant General Richard K. Sutherland; his intelligence chief, German-born Major General Charles A. Willoughby; Rear Admiral Forrest P. Sherman (now Chief of Naval Operations, then representing Admiral Chester Nimitz), and others. Within five hours, straining through interpreters, the Americans found what they wanted to know about harbors, airfields, and minefields, in Japan. Kawabe, arrogant to the last, flashed a wad of American dollar bills, and sent an American soldier out to buy six cartons of cigarettes. Kawabe flew back to Tokyo next day with twenty-five pages of orders from MacArthur.

Then, on September 2, on the broad, sun-warmed deck of the battleship *Missouri,* MacArthur sternly bade the beaten foe to sign the document of unconditional surrender. His voice was heavy with emotion; only a tremor of his hands betrayed his advancing years. For MacArthur it was the supreme moment of his life as a military man.

As MacArthur saw it, in his opening remarks, "the issues, involving divergent ideals and ideologies, have been determined on the battlefields of the world and hence are not for our discussion or debate. Nor is it for us here to meet, representing as we do a majority of the people of the earth, in a spirit of distrust, malice, or hatred. But rather it is for us, both victors and vanquished, to rise to that higher dignity which alone befits the sacred purposes we are about to serve, committing all of our peoples unreservedly to faithful compliance with the undertakings they are here formally to assume."

On the *Missouri* flew the same Stars and Stripes that had flown over the Capitol in Washington on December 7, 1941, the day Pearl Harbor was hit. At MacArthur's side on the deck were two who had known defeat as he had: Lieutenant General Jonathan M. Wainwright, who had stayed behind on Corregidor, and British Lieutenant General Sir Arthur Percival, who had surrendered Singapore. Wainwright had been found about a week before in a Jap prison camp at Mukden, Manchuria, a wraith of what he had been after three years on a rice diet. MacArthur had said when Corregidor fell: "Through the bloody haze of its last reverberating shot I shall always seem to see the vision of its grim, gaunt, and ghostly men."

His opening remarks concluded on the *Missouri's* deck, MacArthur said firmly: "I now invite the representatives of the Emperor of Japan and the Japanese Government and the Japanese Imperial General Headquarters to sign the instrument of surrender at the places indicated."

Up stepped a stumpy-legged Japanese. He looked ridiculous and slightly out of place in the gathering of freshly starched khaki and shining gold braid. He was dressed in top hat, cutaway, and striped trousers, the old-world diplomat to the last degree. He wore an artificial leg, replacing one limb that a Korean bomb had torn off some years before. The Japanese was Mamoru Shigemitsu, Foreign Minister. He signed. Clanking alongside was Lieutenant General Yoshijiro Umezu, decorated to the ears, his samurai sword dangling from his waist. Before them stood MacArthur—open-necked shirt, thin circle of five stars on his collar, gold-braided hat on his head.

It was his moment of triumph, but he took it humbly.

For the Japanese it was disaster, their first real defeat in 2,000 years. For the Allies it was a step into an uneasy, atomic future. Joseph Stalin alone may have known the answers, but he wasn't talking that day.

The only guideposts along the route for MacArthur were these: the Yalta agreement of early 1945; the earlier Cairo Declaration; the Potsdam Proclamation of July 1945; the White House directive to MacArthur of September 1945, and the Moscow Conference communiqué of December 1945.

Cairo limited Japan to sovereignty over the four main islands and some minor ones. Yalta was to bring Russia into the war against Japan within three months after Germany's collapse; the price (sweetening some of the bitter taste of Russia's defeat in 1904): Sakhalin; Dairen, Port Arthur, status quo in Outer Mongolia, China to have "sovereignty" over Manchuria; and the Kurils, north of Japan, to be returned to Russia.

Potsdam called upon the Japanese to surrender unconditionally, without revealing the Yalta commitment that Russia would join the Pacific war. The White House directive gave MacArthur the broad base for democratizing Japan. The Moscow communiqué (by the United States, Russia, and Britain) set up a Far Eastern commission at Washington with limited powers and an Allied council for Japan in Tokyo with purely advisory powers.

No one could mistake the ring of finality and purpose in MacArthur's voice as it flashed around the world from the *Missouri*. Likewise, no one could fathom the terror and despair that gripped 82,000,000 Japanese. What confidence had they left? They had heard Hirohito, their emperor, supposedly the infallible and almighty descendant of the Sun Goddess, tell them via

radio that they had lost the war. Further, he had commanded them: "Hostilities cease forthwith."

The Japanese heard Hirohito by transcription as he
squeaked out his imperial rescript. There was mass weeping. Scores of loyal subjects disemboweled themselves
in the streets before the palace. It was the same sort of
reaction we'd seen on blood-bathed Saipan in July
1944, when hordes of drunken, half-armed Japanese
soldiers swamped our lines, killed a lot of Americans,
then committed suicide. A few days later we had seen
Japanese civilians on Saipan scorning our offers of food
and sanctuary, standing round in circles, praying, then
tossing hand grenades at one another. Others, whole
families of them, jumped into the sea after orgiastic
sessions of bathing, prayers, and song.

There was an alarming jump in the suicide rate in
Tokyo at surrender time. The Japanese had been led
to believe we would come swaggering in, sabering right
and left. (They probably would have done so in the
United States had we lost the war.) Many died by their
own hand, for lack of food, clothing, and shelter. Others
mourned men who would never return from Palau,
Borneo, New Guinea.

A few hotheads, including some Kamikaze pilots who
would never fly again, heard of the Emperor's intention
to order a cease fire by radio. They forced their way into
his palace the morning after he had recorded his rescript, which had been hidden in a small office safe.
They could not find the record, but they shot up the
place and were fired on in return by loyal soldiers.
Thirty-odd were killed on both sides.

Another group approached General Umezu, who was
to sign the surrender for the general staff, suggesting
he lead a *coup d'état*. He refused. The angry rebels

forged arrest warrants for the Emperor's closest advisers. They raided Radio Tokyo, machine-gunned the
Prime Minister's home, set fire to that of the president
of the Privy Council. They wrecked radio transmitting
towers near the city. But they did not find the recording
or keep Hirohito off the air.

Frustrated, and advised of their grave error in violating the palace precincts, many rebels committed suicide. Hirohito went on Radio Tokyo at noon, and it was
all over.

Military resistance was ended. But there remained for
MacArthur the problem of dealing with mental resistance, obstructionism, quiet sabotage of American directives through red tape. There was a slowdown strike
against the occupation. Many Japanese felt they should
have special treatment because they had always been
"democrats" and had obeyed the militarists out of fear.
Others felt that Japan, not having been conquered in
her home islands by actual invasion and because she
had "capitulated" so magnanimously, was entitled to
some sort of special treatment from the conquerors. This
was abundantly evident from conversations with Japanese Foreign Office functionaries in the early weeks of
the occupation; the mayor of atom-bombed Hiroshima
later asserted that America should rebuild his city because it had been the guinea pig for the atom bomb.

The surrender also put on ice in the Pentagon files
two thorough plans for invading Japan. In Operation
Olympic, scheduled for November 1945, the Sixth Army
would have staged a three-pronged invasion of Kyushu,
southernmost main island of Japan. Early in 1946 the
Eighth Army would have struck in Operation Coronet
at the heart of the Japanese Empire, the Kanto plain
around Tokyo.

Either or both jobs would have been bloody. From what we learned afterward, the Japanese, without stock piles of arms and munitions, most of their cities blasted and burned, intended, nevertheless, to fight on with that tenacity which made them tough opponents on every island in the Pacific where they were directly engaged.

General MacArthur has called the initial occupation of Japan by a comparative handful of air-borne troops "one of the greatest gambles of history." What he meant was this: Japan, a relatively unknown country, was an armed hostile camp. Would the Emperor carry conviction to a proud, militaristic people? The frustrated Kamikazes were a doubtful quantity. Snipers might have been ready. No one knew what caches of arms lay in the hills.

But General of the Army George C. Marshall, testifying that we had broken Japanese codes almost throughout the war, was able to say that from our tuning in on Japanese radio chatter between the time of the surrender offer and our actual entry into Japan, we knew we would not be resisted and could take over with a handful of men at first.

One might have expected stealthy stabbings of Americans. There were none. A few Americans were killed in the first five years of the occupation now ending; some Japanese were killed by a few green Americans who had been hitting the bottle a bit hard.

No one would normally expect a vanquished foe to welcome the conqueror like a long-lost brother. Humans are not made that way, especially when they have been at one another's throats for three and a half war years.

Moreover, the Japanese did not like foreigners or

Westerners. They remembered their own propaganda; they remembered the atom bomb.

But there at Atsugi Field in August 1945 were Japanese who poured out excellent beer for the first contingents of Americans and fed them well.

Surrender, complete and unconditional, was the Allied demand. There was only one bargain with Japan, and it was to insure a successful occupation. That bargain was to retain the Emperor. Otherwise, a stern but just peace was framed by MacArthur.

President Truman, reading the Potsdam terms for Japan, warned on August 6, 1945, that "if they do not accept our terms, they may expect a rain of ruin from the air the like of which has never been seen on this earth." The same day the atom bomb hit Hiroshima. Three days later Russia went into the war against Japan.

The very day after Hiroshima, Prime Minister Suzuki, and Foreign Minister Togo (who died last summer) were telling the Emperor to accept the Potsdam terms quickly. There was a final wrangle when leading Japanese objected to the idea that MacArthur would be over the Emperor. But the Emperor did not mind. He seemed relieved.

MacArthur's troops entered a battered, decaying, apathetic Japan. Its tinderbox cities had been razed by B-29 fire raids from Saipan. (When they lost Saipan, the Japanese in authority knew they had lost the war.) The Japanese Navy had been sunk or rendered useless. The merchant fleet had been wiped from the seas, the air force all but destroyed (save for the 5,000 suicide pilots who hoped for a final blow at us). Munitions factories had practically ceased operations for want of raw materials.

Japan was a helpless patient on an operating table awaiting the surgeon's knife. The surgeon was Mac-Arthur.

His choice as Supreme Commander for the Allied Powers (SCAP) in Japan was generally applauded. Nimitz had been the Navy's choice, naturally and commendably. But MacArthur seemed the over-all best choice. He had lived long in the Orient, he knew the oriental mind, he had the manners and presence and bearing of the romantic, hereditary colonial soldier which would do him no harm and actually a lot of good.

To the Japanese he is tall, erect, handsome, and always correct; his step firm; his jaw jutting, his eyes clear and steady; his dress impeccable; his grasp of military and political history remarkable; his charm and compelling personality unmistakable. He was and is the sort of leader that Winston Churchill was for so many years to the British.

And MacArthur, with prescience, had no illusions about the popularity of the occupation army he commanded. He foresaw that it would outlive its welcome in three to five years, and he felt that then it should go home or at least retire to strictly military bases in Japan or near by. He knew of the irritations that even a benevolent conqueror can set up, but he intended to stay on in Tokyo until a peace treaty had been concluded.

One wonders whether MacArthur, standing on the *Missouri's* deck and hearing the pens scratch signatures on the surrender document, cast his thoughts back ninety-two years. For the table on which the surrender was signed had been used by another American, Commodore Matthew C. Perry, in opening Japan to the West. Perry had a letter, an offer of friendship from President Millard Fillmore, but he was ready to come ashore and use force if necessary to get the letter to the Emperor, who was praying to his Shinto heaven for help. Perry had his way in February 1854.

Atsugi, where MacArthur landed, was about seven miles from Yokohama, where Perry had landed. Mac-Arthur soon had the White House directive, which said to the other Allies that in case of disagreement on Japan, American policy would prevail.

The directive stated the ultimate objectives of the United States. These were, briefly, that we intended to insure that Japan would never again menace the United States or the peace of the world, that a peaceful and responsible government would be formed which would respect the rights of other states and support American objectives as reflected in the United Nations charter. The directive said the Allies did not intend to impose upon Japan a government not supported by the freely expressed will of the people. The Cairo plan for cutting Japan down to the four main islands was restated. Japan was to be completely disarmed and demilitarized, militarism eradicated forever. Freedom of speech, religion, assembly, and press—such fundamental human rights—would be encouraged. So would an economy to meet Japan's peacetime requirements. Hirohito was to be subject to MacArthur, but MacArthur was not committed to support him or anyone else who might oppose "evolutionary changes." (The Japanese were frantic when the first cables garbled "evolutionary" to "revolutionary.")

The secret police were to be dissolved. The ultra-nationalists and militarists would be purged. War criminals would be rounded up. The educational system would be revamped. Financial and economic oligarchies would be broken up. Reparations would be paid; restitution would be made for war loot.

This was a large order to impose upon a country that we knew little about. But MacArthur had a superb sense of timing. He played the occupation by ear. He knew when to act. He never hit the Japanese with too many directives at once. There was a "blizzard" of directives at first, but they were spaced out. Moreover, MacArthur kept the Japanese wondering what might come next; he created a psychology of fear, awe, and wonderment.

MacArthur supplied to the Japanese what they had lacked in the past: leadership. He made the corner policeman a servant of the people, not their master. He abolished thought control and the secret police. He proclaimed freedom of thought; he made it good by springing the Japanese Communists from the jails in which they had languished for as much as fifteen years; he permitted the number-one Red, Sanzo Nosaka, a Moscow-trained agitator, to return from tutelage in Asia.

MacArthur proceeded to wipe out the Black Dragon and other secret societies which were breeding grounds for militarism and the police state. He began to house-clean the Japanese press, screening out with censorship the vestiges of feudal militaristic thought and encouraging editors to comment on and criticize, if they liked, what had been going on in their country. Later he permitted reasonable criticism of the occupation. MacArthur even included the Emperor system as a topic for free discussion. He believed that if it could not stand the test of free discussion, it was not worth retaining.

A new constitution was drafted, primarily at his headquarters, in 1946. Under it the Japanese swore off war, stripped themselves forever of an army and navy and air force, revitalized their Diet (Parliament), and cut the Emperor down to size, making him a constitutional monarch on the British model. He was no longer supreme.

He also tackled Japan's economics in encouraging democratic growths. He ordered the dissolution of the Zaibatsu families, the closely knit clans that held the controls of Japanese industry and finance, and told them to turn their controlling stocks and bonds over for resale to the public, or to workers in subsidiary industries of the Zaibatsu combines.

Strict financial reforms were also on MacArthur's program. He wiped out a great burden of military pensions that had wrecked the budget for years and had fostered a class of do-nothing ex-soldiers. He squeezed war profits from dozens of big firms and hit even the Emperor's multimillion-dollar holdings.

His roundup of war criminals reached right into the imperial household; no one knew for certain in the last months of 1945 whether MacArthur, if he had the evidence, would grab the Emperor.

He undertook a large-scale reform of the school system, purging teachers, throwing out militaristic textbooks. This was sabotaged in the provinces by wily Japanese. In order really to free Japanese minds from feudalistic concepts and open them to Western literature and ideas, MacArthur also fostered the use of Romaji, or Roman letters, to replace the exceedingly difficult ideographs, or picture writing, in which Japanese had been written for centuries. To illustrate: the language had about 60,000 characters, of which an average man might master 10,000 in his lifetime. The newspapers had settled for 5,000 to 6,000 standard ideographs, of which the man in the street who tried to grasp world affairs could probably not understand more than 2,000 to 3,000. Most newspapers, therefore, employed "side writ-

ing," or explanatory notes, alongside the main body of
a news story, to try to tell the reader what it was really
about. So much for the vaunted Japanese "literacy."

A basic concept of democracy for Japan, MacArthur
said, was land reform. He ordered the freeing of farms
and farmers from their slavery; he said no democracy
existed which did not spring from the soil, as in America.
He ordered large landholdings broken up for resale, at
controlled prices, to farmers who had been tenants and
share croppers. MacArthur here clearly understood that
the basis of the unrest in the Orient was lack of control
of land by those who worked it by the sweat of their
brows for absentee landlords.

MacArthur further ordered new elections to the Diet
for early in 1946; these were the first free elections in
Japan and the first in which women members were
given a seat. MacArthur also had given women the
right to vote for the first time.

The General also struck at the heart of old ways in
Japan by having the Emperor, on New Year's Day,
1946, read a rescript over the radio in which he con-
ceded he was not of divine origin.

The Japanese, who are great imitators as well as
idolators, quickly picked up MacArthur as a new deity.
Finally one of their own newspapers had to admonish
the public to stop thinking of him as a god. But to the
Japanese in the early years of the occupation Mac-
Arthur could do no wrong. They liked his aloofness, his
crisp air of finality, his determination, his purposeful-
ness. They admired his long black Cadillac; they admired the firm way he strode out to it from his headquarters twice a day.

MacArthur struck one of his greatest blows at the old
order by abolishing State Shinto. This was a state re-

ligion, much as Naziism in Germany and Fascism in Italy. It was compounded in Japan of pagan mythology, oriental hocus-pocus. It surrounded the imperial line descending from Jimmu, the first emperor, who took the throne in 660 B.C. Originally Shinto was nature worship; in modern Japan it had been corrupted to a state-supported and state-controlled religion that was a useful tool for militarists. It taught that Japan, its emperors, and its people were of divine origin, that Japan was an earthly extension of heaven, all other dynasties were mortal, Japan would one day rule the world. The people were taxed for support of this so-called religion. It was woven into their lives. Its priesthood was government appointed and controlled.

With a stroke of his pen MacArthur outlawed State Shinto on December 15, 1945. But it was not to die too quickly.

MacArthur has always been a target for uninformed critics. He was the "D'Artagnan of the A.E.F.," the "polished popinjay" of prewar Washington. His long-time antagonist as Chief of Staff in Washington was one Representative Ross Collins, Democrat, of Mississippi, who became chairman of the House Appropriations Committee.

Collins used to say: "MacArthur wants a Chinese army—a lot of men and low firepower."

In October 1945 the critics were hitting at Mac-Arthur again; from Washington, as usual. The scheme for a Far Eastern commission for Japan, with technical veto power over MacArthur, was being broached. He let it be known that if any nation, particularly Russia, had veto power over him he would go home.

The critics thought MacArthur was being too soft;

that he was running a "kid-glove" occupation. By coincidence, MacArthur summoned seventy-three-year-old Premier Baron Shidehara, and told him bluntly to get busy on reforming the social order. He told Shidehara to install suffrage for women, freedom of speech and religion, liberalization of schools, democratization of industry, and unionization of labor.

"Unquestionably," said MacArthur, "this will involve a liberalization of the constitution."

Stalling, the Japanese named Prince Konoye, to form within the office of the Marquis Kido, keeper of the Privy Seal—another who was nabbed as a suspected war criminal—a commission to study the constitution. Konoye was disavowed publicly by MacArthur; he committed suicide on the eve of his arrest as a war criminal.

The new constitution was finally unveiled on March 6, 1946. MacArthur was justly proud of it and said he would not change a comma to please the Russians or anyone else. (The Russians claimed that the constitution was a job reserved for all the Allies.)

The constitution, now in effect, is modeled on the written one of the United States and the unwritten one of Great Britain. But it renounced war "forever" and banned all military forces.

It made Hirohito a constitutional monarch, British style. It made the parliament supreme and the cabinet responsible to the parliament. It instituted a bill of rights. It put sovereignty ultimately in the hands of the Japanese people.

If MacArthur did nothing else for Japan, he gave its people a charter of liberty.

11. MacArthur and the Oriental Mind

As General MacArthur's plane *Bataan* climbed into the clouds and headed for Korea, the General began to pace the runway between the seats ("he always walks half the way on every flight we make," commented his pilot later), dug into his pockets for his corncob and, turning to the correspondents, said: "I don't smoke this back there in Tokyo; they'd think I was a farmer."

MacArthur has never once appeared to be a farmer to the Japanese; he is held in awesome idolatrous respect and in some ways, through no fault of his own, he is revered even more than Hirohito. This did not just happen. The regard with which he is held by the Japanese is a direct result of his complete grasp of the oriental mind. Colonel R. C. Kramer, head of the Scientific and Economics Section at the beginning of the occupation, put it this way: "MacArthur keeps one ear glued tight to the ground."

His knowledge of the Far East and his sensitive understanding of the oriental mind are probably his greatest weapons in dealing with the Japanese. That he is accepted by them is proved by the thousands of letters he receives from Japanese in all walks of life. Mothers beg him to father sons for them "so that they shall be

American democratic too." The prostitutes in a body once asked for a union: "Please can we have a union too? We're simply working girls." A Buddhist priest, pretender to Hirohito's throne, wrote that "My throne was deprived me 554 years ago." Letters arrive night and day; some come through the mails, some are left by people who have journeyed from outlying provinces so that their grievances will be heard. So great is this influx that one whole department at supreme head-quarters does nothing else but answer letters. A condensation of this correspondence is read by MacArthur and often action results after investigation.

Never before in Japan's history have the people been given this measure of freedom; never before have they had anybody to appeal to; never before have they had a leader try to understand their problem. And while all aspects of the occupation may not be perfect, Mac-Arthur's superb psychological handling of the occupation so far accounts for his having achieved so much in such a short time.

MacArthur is not superhuman; he makes just as many mistakes as the next person. He has made many during the last five years in Japan. But his batting average has been high, and his real genius shows in the psychological game of chess he has been playing with the Japanese not only since the beginning of the occupation, but indeed since Pearl Harbor.

As far as MacArthur is concerned it is something more than "when in Rome live like the Romans." It is a concentrated study of the way the Oriental lives, works, and, above all, thinks. Yet privately he insists that "even after fifty years of living among these people I still do not understand them." But his whole career in the Orient makes that statement a contradiction in terms. He has studied the folklore of the people; read their military, political, and economic histories. This constant study, plus his practical experience, has given MacArthur a greater understanding of the oriental mind than possibly any other living American statesman or soldier.

He has made this study a life's work, and his every move seems to be predicated, *not on what the Western world will think,* as so many of his critics would have us believe, but rather *on what the Oriental will think.* For MacArthur has repeatedly pointed out that Occidentals should not compare their reasoning or interpretation of values with the Oriental and expect it to come out equal. The War Department fully realized this ability of MacArthur years ago.

What will the Japanese think of this action? Can this directive, very much necessary to the occupation, be put into effect without the Japanese losing face? How can we circumvent the usual palaver quickly and easily? This and a hundred more questions have to be thought of by MacArthur before any move can be made. He has had to deal gently with the Japanese, yet the occupation has not been a tame affair by any means. A blunt, harsh occupation, an occupation without an effort to understand the people might have proved disastrous. Every closet might now contain a sword, every well a rifle. The Japanese learned quickly that MacArthur had one wish: to show them a democratic way of life; to raise them above the serfdom of centuries. This he is well on the way to completing.

It must be understood that much of MacArthur's actions and utterances have been for the oriental mind only and *not* for consumption by the Western world. If we are to judge MacArthur's actions by Western standards, each move must seem silly, pompous, and indeed stupid. For example, take the extremely controversial saying of the General's, "I shall return!"

Psychological experts today say that that one phrase struck more terror into the hearts of the Japanese than any other single psychological warfare effort throughout the whole Pacific war. Over and over that one slogan was driven home. It was as nerve-racking to the Japanese as the European variety thought up by Mr. Churchill, the three dots and the long dash spelling out slowly V for victory which was repeated in drumbeats every available moment on all radio bands of the B.B.C. Unfortunately "I shall return" became synonymous with some of the less attractive sides of MacArthur's extraordinary personality.

That same slogan served as a rallying call to the Filipinos. General Carlos P. Romulo, President of the United Nations, says that the phrase "served as a promise and command to the Philippine peoples. They knew his word was his bond."

All over the Pacific on Japanese-held islands the words "I shall return" mysteriously appeared on walls, doors—even on parade grounds—in white paint. Thousands of small white sheets of paper bearing just the three-word sentence began to appear in Japanese files, books, and in supply cases. There is one story of how a Japanese unit in the Philippines broke open a case of shells in the middle of an action and on each shell was neatly stenciled the famous pronouncement. Air-force planes and submarines supplied thousands of match-boxes, playing cards, colored buttons, chewing gum, and even money bearing the message to guerrilla fighters on Japanese-held islands. The Japanese command reluctantly admitted, with the ending of hostilities, that this war of nerves weakened morale among the troops; in fact it gave them a bad case of jitters.

Furthermore, MacArthur had an extremely nasty habit—as far as the Japanese were concerned—of telling their high command exactly where he was going to attack and then doing it. This befuddled the Japanese. Nothing they seemed to do could stop the relentless march of MacArthur's men. Yet they were being told in advance of the next move, and each move bore out the saying, "I shall return." This probably explains why the Japanese never belittled MacArthur in their broadcasts during the war. Tokyo Rose, for example, never once handled MacArthur with anything but kid gloves. MacArthur, on the other hand, scorned and belittled the Japanese commanders and called them stupid; he criticized their military tactics to such an extent that he forced several high-ranking officers to lose face before their men. This, of course, was precisely what the propaganda was intended to do.

Enemy intelligence and psychological warfare go hand in hand, but MacArthur has always disliked intelligence reports. He once went on record with this: "Only 95 per cent of all intelligence is accurate; the other 5 per cent depends entirely on the evaluation of the commanding general." Perhaps this explains his dislike of the O.S.S. even though it was directed by a former Rainbow Division officer, an old and good friend of MacArthur, Colonel William (Wild Bill) Donovan. The O.S.S. once suggested an idea to MacArthur which did not quite meet with his ideas of psychological warfare—simply because he did not believe that it would work. The idea was that several hundred foxes, daubed with phosphorescent paint, be released just before American troops landed on the Japanese mainland.

This move, it was felt, would cause great confusion because of the Japanese superstitution that "a ghostly fox seen at night carries an evil spirit." This was all very well, but the General who knew what landings were like figured that the salt water would wash off most of the paint. The O.S.S. tried out the scheme in Chesapeake Bay just to find out if MacArthur was right. The foxes were released from a landing barge and swam ashore. Most of the paint came off en route. Then the foxes calmly sat down on the beach and licked off the remainder.

MacArthur's greatest psychological gamble was the initial occupation of Japan made by only a handful of armed men. He felt that the Japanese would respect the surrender of the Emperor Hirohito. Yet it seemed like dropping out of the sky into a vast armed camp of 82,000,000 people, who for all anybody knew might have been preparing a hot reception. The decision to do this was MacArthur's and MacArthur's alone. True, he had been promised by the Japanese emissaries in Manila that there would be no opposition to the landing of troops. Yet it was still "one of the greatest gambles in history," as it has since been called.

The occupation army in Japan at no time ever exceeded 200,000 men—except at the very beginning, when units which had been fighting through the Pacific converged on Japan at the end of the hostilities. This occupation force was to control some 82,000,000 people—a population of more than half that of the United States. MacArthur's shrewd handling of the Japanese people saved him another 1,800,000 men. He reasoned that control of Japan lay with control of the Emperor and the Imperial Institution. Without the Emperor he once said "we would have needed a force of two million men."

MacArthur's own psychological warfare experts had held during the war that one of the first acts of the occupation was that Hirohito should be immediately treated as a war criminal. Brigadier General Bonner Fellers, head of psychological warfare in the Pacific during the war, and later military secretary to MacArthur, wrote of Hirohito shortly before the occupation began that "as Emperor and acknowledged head of the State, Hirohito cannot sidestep war guilt. He is part of and must be considered an instigator of the Pacific war . . . whether or not Pearl Harbor was against the Emperor's will is of little consequence . . . inescapably he is responsible."

After MacArthur landed in Japan he didn't see it quite that way; he made no direct move to oust Hirohito. This negative procedure ran counter to the desires of the Chinese, Australians, New Zealanders, and of course the Russians. They frankly wanted the Emperor out and named a war criminal. MacArthur said no.

His reasoning went something like this: Let's remove all the trappings surrounding the Emperor and the Imperial Institution such as State Shintoism and the thraldom of militarists such as Konoye, Tojo, *et al.;* let's prove to the Japanese people that he is not a god, that he is not divine, and then let's see just what sort of Emperor he would make if given the reins. MacArthur warned, however: "Let's not martyrize the Emperor; in their good time the Japanese will whittle him down to size."

It worked. For months, as the ax swept closer to Hirohito, as one top adviser after another was grabbed and tried as a war criminal, MacArthur let the Emperor sweat it out, wondering all the time if he wouldn't be next. These moves plus the issuing of MacArthur's "Four Freedoms" directive turned the pitiless spotlight of publicity onto the Imperial Institution. For the first time the once blindly obedient millions of Japanese began to question Hirohito's authority, his descent, his supposed divinity.

MacArthur's acute understanding of the Japanese, his very aloofness, indeed his physical stature, lent all these moves great theater. To the Japanese the war had simply stopped. They never felt that they had been beaten. For the first time many millions of Japanese began to realize that they had been really trounced and here was MacArthur to prove it.

Had the Japanese refused to co-operate, had the hard crust of the remaining militarists been given any loose rein at all, MacArthur would have had to enforce his every move with troops. He continually kept the Japanese off balance as he played for time.

His greatest stroke occurred on January 1, 1946. The Chaplinesque Hirohito, who claimed descent unbroken for ages from Japan's feudal gods—the oriental counterparts of the Hitler-revived Wotan and Thor—climbed shakily onto the podium in the Japanese Diet and read his New Year's message to the Japanese people in which he calmly told them that he was not divine and, what was more, he never had been. He declared that the conception was "false." Furthermore, his subjects were told flatly that they were not superior to other races nor were they fated "to bring the eight corners of the world under one roof"—a Japanese roof. Hirohito did not think of all this himself; neither did his advisers. The speech, it is suspected, was written at MacArthur's headquarters by none other than the General himself.

Had MacArthur at that time made this announcement the Japanese would not have believed him. Today they would. The Japanese believed what their Emperor told them; a curtain was lifted, a curtain which had kept their every thought, word, and action in serfdom for centuries.

Such an admission by the Emperor during the war might have caused a tremendous social and moral upheaval in Japan, for the myth of Hirohito's divinity, fostered through years by the state religion of Shintoism and nurtured by Tojo and all the other modern shoguns who ever held the Emperor in their grip, was something that no Japanese had dared to question.

Now the myth was exploded without a ripple. The upper-crust Japanese—those who with Tojo and Konoye among others had used Hirohito's "divinity" to keep the rank and file under control—said they knew all along the Emperor was not of divine descent. But, they added, "it wasn't a bad thing for the people to believe."

It was a sort of opiate, this emperor worship. Japan's emperors had always been mouthpieces for the militarists, chauvinists, and other members of the tight little clique of rulers who had controlled and planned Japan's aggressions. Hirohito was no exception. He issued for Tojo the Imperial Rescript that formally declared war on the United States. He knew and approved in advance the general plans for the attack on Pearl Harbor, for all of Japan's major expansionist moves in the Far East. Now the shoe was on the other foot. MacArthur, in the first year of the occupation, used Hirohito as a mouthpiece until such time as he had swung the Japanese over to the belief in the possibility of the resurgence of a new Japan along democratic lines.

Another example of MacArthur's understanding of the oriental mind was his commanding the Emperor to come before him. If ever an emperor lost face before his people, Hirohito did at this time. Just what the Japanese expected Hirohito to do is not quite clear. In fact, their conception of the occupation is not clear. They met the troops with cameras and great beaming welcomes. They soon found out that the occupation under MacArthur was not going to be a picnic. And the first person who came to this realization was Hirohito.

Wearing an ancient morning suit, silk topper, and striped pants, Hirohito and his chief adviser (at that time the Marquis Kido, who a few days later was led off to a cold cell as a war criminal) stepped out of an early-vintage Daimler to pay their respects to MacArthur.

They were escorted into the embassy. As they walked through the door, the Marquis Kido was politely asked to step into an anteroom. For one awful moment Hirohito realized that he was alone. Kido couldn't believe that anybody would treat the Emperor of Japan in such a manner. He tried to protest. Everybody was just oh, so polite. "The Supreme Commander wishes to talk to the Emperor alone," Kido was told. So the man behind the throne cooled his heels while timorous, shabby Hirohito walked with uncertain steps down the hall into the study. Never before had he been without an adviser; never before had he been asked to do any real thinking for himself. Always it had been Kido or some other stooge who had answered for him with "The Emperor feels that . . ." or "The Emperor, after great consideration . . ." Nobody had ever left him alone before.

MacArthur's aides later said that the General sensed that Hirohito had never been allowed to think for himself. So now we find him walking down the passage to MacArthur's study. A door is opened. He walks into the room, and there stands MacArthur. Just what happened between them MacArthur has never said, but photographs show the tall, simply dressed MacArthur (he wore an open-necked shirt, ordinary officer's issue suntan trousers, no mark of rank or decoration) towering over the startled-looking Hirohito. The Japanese lost face simply because Hirohito lost face.

Some idea of the terror which gripped this "Emperor without peer on the land, the sea, and in the air; the direct descendent of the Sun Goddess Amaterasu," can best be shown by his puny political and childlike effort at public relations which he later tried (without informing his advisers) on Robert Patterson. Patterson, then Secretary of War, arrived in Japan sometime later. For some strange reason Hirohito—whose fate still hung in the balance, so he thought—decided that Patterson might be able to save him, or at least influence those in authority to have mercy on him. One night, as Patterson was dining with MacArthur, a messenger left a parcel for Mr. Patterson. It was a solid-gold cigarette case with an inscription. Patterson sent it back—immediately. There was no balm to Hirohito's troubled mind here.

The Japanese, too, were worried about their Emperor—especially the upper crust, the "old-school kimono" boys. They knew that MacArthur was not committed to permanent retention of Hirohito. The broad directive from the White House, issued in September 1945, specifically said that the Supreme Commander could change the government machinery or personnel or act directly if the Emperor or anyone else did not satisfactorily meet the requirements of General MacArthur in putting the surrender terms into effect.

"The policy," the directive added, "does not commit the Supreme Commander to support the Emperor or any other Japanese governmental authority in opposition to evolutionary changes looking toward the attainment of the United States objectives."

The unhappy task of finding out Hirohito's exact status with the Supreme Commander went to his new adviser, the Marquis Matsudaira, who had taken over the post in the absence of Marquis Kido, who now languished behind bars. (Kido: "I wish to lodge a formal complaint—there is no heat whatsoever in this prison." General Eichelberger: "I fully agree, it is a disgraceful state of affairs. You fellows should have had heating installed when our boys were prisoners here.")

Matsudaira is a fairly tall, thin, aristocratic type, a descendant of one of Japan's oldest and most powerful feudal families. In the past he had great influence. Now things were—to put it mildly—rather different. How do you approach a conqueror and ask whether he's going to hang the Emperor or not without losing face? You can't just ring him up or make an appointment to ask him the question. Then, no matter what his answer, you still lose face. This question must have passed through Matsudaira's mind, for his method of approach was typically oriental; it has been used, with variations, a thousand times in the last five years of the occupation.

Hirohito's adviser summoned the Foreign Office's number-one "smoothie," a Princeton-educated, oily character who had broadcast propaganda to the Allied troops during the war—"I was forced to do it, y'know, but I really never believed a word I was saying"—by the name of Kase. He was ordered to pass along the word that Hirohito's new adviser would like to entertain Brigadier General Thorpe, head of SCAP's counter-intelligence, at a geisha dinner.

Thorpe has always had a nose for excitement and new developments. "About thirty years ago I planned a trip to Java and I checked with the War Department, for some of its intelligence files. I found two articles from the *National Geographic* and nothing more, so ever since I have been finding things out for myself," he once said. It was not hard to persuade Thorpe to attend.

The dinner was in excellent taste. Thorpe enjoyed the meal, as did everybody else. Geisha girls fluttered back and forth across the highly polished floor with the various courses; hot, bitter-sweet sake appeared as though by magic to refill the delicate china bowls placed conveniently in front of each guest. It took Matsudaira a long time to come to the point. Hirohito's adviser, after some superb needling by General Thorpe, came out with it. He indicated that the Emperor was worried. The directives were getting harsher. Did the General think . . . . Well, would MacArthur grab Hirohito? How could the Emperor save himself?

General Thorpe suddenly became exceedingly interested in his food; he would not bite. If he knew that MacArthur might name the Emperor on the next war-criminal list he did not say so. He gave the retort courteously and diplomatically: the Emperor's future was up to himself and to the Japanese people. If anyone had a guilty conscience about the past, it was his own fault.

He told Matsudaira very bluntly that nothing could save the Imperial Institution if Japan was to be run along the same old lines. He advised the Emperor and his government to get busy and do something about the plight of the people and not sit around all day bewailing the sternness of MacArthur's directives. He told him also that there had been monarchies in France and elsewhere which had been swept away on the tide of revolution simply because of oppressive conditions and "do-nothing-ism" as existed in Japan. If such a revolution came in Japan, General Thorpe warned, no one could stop it, not even the occupation forces. Moreover, they would not try to stop it unless their own safety was in peril.

"If you Japanese love your Emperor so much," General Thorpe added, "why don't you get to work and make of him a genuine, worth-while being?"

"But how?" asked Matsudaira.

So the General handed out the prescription.

He said the Emperor had never acted human, that he was too aloof from his people, particularly when the people were down on their uppers, and that he ought to mix more in public and to indulge frankly in some un-Japanese public relations. The meeting ended on this note. Matsudaira was still very much in the dark, but he had been given something to think about.

In the early months the Japanese, born imitators that they are, tried hard to be more American than the Americans. Hirohito was no exception. Prompted by his old guard, who urged him to seek a good press, correspondents were invited to a duck hunt in the Imperial Palace grounds. This failed miserably, too, for the correspondents were treated to the most sumptuous meal—everything from caviar to "brandied guinea hen in aspic"—they had ever seen in Japan or elsewhere. Outside the palace walls three quarters of Tokyo's population was starving.

It took Hirohito and his ilk a long time to learn; a long time to think for themselves without the constant prodding of MacArthur. The army of occupation was wooed with parties and entertainment of every sort. This "kill with kindness" plan included such items as "Friendship Houses" with assembly-line staging. Prostitutes operated twenty-four hours out of the twenty-four. MacArthur would have none of that. Gradually it dawned on the Japanese promoters of this sort of thing that they had better toe the line or else. MacArthur was swift and harsh where he had to be, but he always followed one theory: the Japanese people in good time will whittle down not only Hirohito but also the die-hards.

Today in the new Japan the people are their own masters, no longer dominated by a rubber-stamp government. Of course there is still a long way to go. The Japanese have still to produce a post-war leader, but Hirohito is now trying to be an emperor. His people respect him, they are loyal to him. There it ends. He is simply a figurehead. This insignificant little man now kisses babies, opens flower shows, and acts like a good Tammany Hall politician. Indeed it is not surprising nowadays to find him wading in the surf, his trousers rolled above his knees—still wearing the fedora—playing with the children on the beach. He still collects mosses and lichens; he still writes fantastic poetry. Lately it seems happier. Perhaps this little item is significant of the trend of events in Japan. Around Hirohito's palace there is a well-stocked moat containing mostly carp. These have always been the Emperor's private property and only by royal decree were special friends of his allowed to fish for the carp, which, incidentally, were considered "sacred." It is actually on record that several Japanese many years ago were executed for daring to cast a line into the waters. Today Japan's Joe Doakes (Susukisan) fish the moat. Hirohito, too, was tied by the militarists. MacArthur once said: "Hirohito was so controlled by the militarists that he nearly had to get permission to go to the bathroom." Times have changed.

Today there is less than one division of troops, and an

undersized division at that, in Japan. All units that could be spared were rushed to the front, and there, as this book goes to press, they are being hotly engaged. It would seem on the face of it that here is the Kremlin's chance to call on Japan's Communists and the thousands of Soviet-indoctrinated Japanese prisoners of war, who returned to their homes only within the last two years, to strike now while MacArthur's hands are tied. Furthermore, what remains of the old guard in Japan might well welcome the idea. General MacArthur is gambling again; he believes in the Japanese people. And it would appear that they believe in him.

12. MacArthur and the Russians

The Three-power Conference at Yalta early in 1945 "marked the high tide of British, Russian, and American co-operation on the war and the post-war settlement." So said the late Edward R. Stettinius, Jr., then Secretary of State. Many American newspapers echoed him. And that was understandable. East and West had shed their blood against Hitler. We were comrades at arms; we would never be comrades in arms.

An intended song that was never fully written or performed at one of the recent Gridiron Dinners in Washington would have had the late Franklin D. Roosevelt, cigarette holder and all, on the stage and phrasing these opening lyrics to the tune of "Let Me Call You Sweetheart":

> Yalta, Yalta, Yalta,
> Winston, Joe, and I
> Yalta, Yalta, Yalta,
> Just a Russian lull—a—bye!

That, of course, was a hindsight view—but rather acute—of the situation that the United States and Great Britain handed to Douglas MacArthur in the emotional flush of victory.

In 1943 Stalin said Russia would go to war against

Japan. He said so to Cordell Hull, then Secretary of State. He said the same thing to President Roosevelt and to Winston Churchill at Teheran not long afterward. A year later he repeated it to Churchill, W. Averell Harriman, our Lend-Lease expediter, and others. Three months after Germany's defeat, said Stalin, Russia would be in, against Japan . . . provided there had been an agreement with China.

Not until the Yalta talks were half over did Stettinius learn at second hand from Harriman and from Harry Hopkins—in effect the "number-two President"—that Russia's entry into the Japanese war had even been discussed. Stettinius wrote that he then asked President Roosevelt whether there was anything the State Department should pursue about the Japanese question. President Roosevelt said it was primarily a military matter.

The next thing that the Secretary of State knew, the Yalta agreement was out. Russia agreed to enter the war against Japan on several conditions:

The status quo in Outer Mongolia was to be preserved—to Russia's advantage.

Avenging the Russian defeat at Japan's hands in 1904, Russia would get Sakhalin, Dairen, Port Arthur, and effective control over the Chinese-Eastern and South Manchurian Railroad.

Russia would also get the Kuril Islands, pointed like a dagger at the heart of Japan.

The Yalta bargain on Japan was secret—top secret. It was rushed to Washington and put into President Roosevelt's personal safe. Stettinius never saw it. It may prove to have been the greatest single argument against secret covenants secretly arrived at. Not even the Chinese were told about it; but, then, they were always sort of a fifth wheel among the "Big Five."

Mr. Stettinius has made it clear that the Yalta deal on Japan was dictated by military considerations. Secretary of War Stimson related that the United States would have thrown 5,000,000 men, soldiers, sailors, and airmen, against Japan in the final invasion and fully expected casualties on the order of 1,000,000. Hence any help was welcome.

A few months later Russia hedged on those parts of the Yalta agreement that related to the Balkans. Our military again advised patience, wrote Mr. Stettinius, lest Russia's entry against Japan be endangered. Japan was believed to be very strong in Manchuria, where Russian troops would engage the Japanese; yet at Yalta, China was to keep Manchuria. Mr. Stettinius says that the President did not agree to Red control of Manchuria, nor did he agree to Russia's entry into northern Korea. "Actually," Mr. Stettinius wrote, "Russian entrance into northern Korea was agreed to, after Yalta, by American military authorities as part of the taking of the surrender of Japanese troops."

The Russians bagged upward of 400,000 Japanese troops in Korea and Manchuria, many of them in crack units that had been ready for a tough fight against the Reds when Hirohito figuratively blew the whistle that ended the war.

And the issue of the Jap prisoners of war was to become one of the stumbling blocks to any co-operation between Douglas MacArthur and the Russians in the occupation of Japan.

MacArthur was under no illusions about the Reds when he became Supreme Commander for the Allies. Just as he used to talk during World War I of "the Boche," he now began to talk of "the Muscovite bulging his muscles and lusting for power." No doubt he had also heard of the reports that there had been sharp words between Foreign Secretary Molotov and Averell Harriman over MacArthur's projected appointment. The official Russian news agency, Tass, found it necessary to deny this and said that Russia favored a control council for Japan made up of Russian, American, Chinese, and British representatives with an American as permanent chairman. Stalin is reported to have reminded Harriman that if the United States had an overriding interest in Japan, it was parallel to Soviet interest in the Balkan States.

The Russians accepted MacArthur, but they flatly refused to send any occupation troops to Japan because they would have been subject to his over-all authority. They tried hard to send a force with a Russian general as their only boss, but it did not work.

MacArthur made it plain, too, that the Allied Council for Japan (which held its first meeting on April 5, 1946) and the Far Eastern Commission in Washington were going to be purely advisory to him. His headquarters had not been kept informed in advance of the setting up of these agencies and of the exact limits of their jurisdiction, and it was understandable that MacArthur, through a spokesman, put out word in Tokyo that if he wasn't going to be the Supreme Commander in fact as well as in name, he was going to "quit and go home." MacArthur had no intention of sitting around Tokyo as a super military policeman while someone else, presumably diplomats in striped pants, sent him orders.

At the very first meeting of the Allied Council in Tokyo, MacArthur, in his welcoming speech, laid down the law. He said:

"As the functions of the council will be advisory and consultative, it will not divide the heavy administrative responsibility of the Supreme Commander as the sole executive authority for the Allied powers in Japan, but it will make available to him the several viewpoints of its members on questions of policy and action."

MacArthur stressed his position as sole authority in 3,000 words and let the council members know also that "the purposes of the occupation are now well advanced." He then took his leave, saying he would be too busy to sit in on all council meetings but would send a deputy.

That deputy at first was the late George Atcheson Jr., whom the State Department had sent out to Japan in the fall of 1945 to serve as diplomatic and political adviser to MacArthur. Atcheson, who lost his life in the "ditching" of a transport plane in the Pacific, always had to communicate with the State Department via MacArthur's headquarters and the War Department in Washington. At least that had the merit of preventing crossed wires.

MacArthur kept the council busy and in its place. Its sessions were held at a round, well-polished table in the Meiji Building, not far from the Dai Ichi Building in which he had his own headquarters. The council met about twice a month for an all-day session that was interrupted only for lunch.

MacArthur had set the formula for the council at the very first meeting: what they could not do. Thereafter the delegates tried to break down that formula. They never did. They were so bad-tempered, sitting around all day and looking at one another, that W. Mac-Mahon Ball, of Australia, representing the British Commonwealth, said plaintively that he "could see no need for this council at all."

It was just as bad with the Far Eastern Commission in Washington. They held lengthy meetings, and set up many committees in the ornate old Japanese embassy on Connecticut Avenue. But in Washington it wasn't MacArthur who had the Indian sign on them; it was the Russian delegate and his entourage. The commission would ask for Russia's views on certain points. The Russian delegate would say that he would have to refer the point to Moscow. He would do so—by mail. After two months he might get an answer: they were awfully busy in Moscow and would try to find him the real answer later.

At the fifth council session in Tokyo, MacArthur, playing things expertly by ear, threw the members into a tizzy by suddenly asking their opinion on seventeen urgent problems. Mr. Atcheson apologetically said that MacArthur would continue to seek the council's advice by laying important matters before them "in a growing number if this does not overburden the council." These seventeen items were a terrible strain on the redheaded interpreter who served the Russian delegate.

The top Russian on the council was Lieutenant General Kuzma N. Derevyanko. He was a great needler of MacArthur when he could get close to the General. But MacArthur caught him beautifully one day: American military policemen picked up the Russian for reckless driving. Derevyanko was released when his identity was established, but in Russian fashion he rushed a demand to MacArthur for an apology. MacArthur asked the M.P.: "Was the Russian violating the law?"

"Yes, sir!" replied the M.P.

"Then you can tell him," declared MacArthur, "there will be no apology."

Derevyanko is said to have asked: "Did MacArthur say that?" He was assured. Slapping his leg, the Russian roared gleefully:

"What a man!"

From time to time the Far Eastern Commission in Washington—with eleven members, not four as in Tokyo, sitting around the table—would respectfully ask MacArthur to send a liaison officer from his command. This, said MacArthur, could not be done because the Supreme Commander "has given his personal attention to this question and there is no officer in a position to express in detail his views."

At one point the Far Eastern Commission stated publicly that there was "no effort, either by the Far Eastern Commission or the United States Government, to take issue with General MacArthur."

About seven months after its first meeting the council in Tokyo had just about run out of things to talk about. MacArthur told it, in effect: "Since you do not wish to take up the questions submitted by me, you must submit your own from here on."

MacArthur knew he was on firm ground, but he did not forget to be gracious. Despite the constant strife with Derevyanko, both MacArthur and Mr. Atcheson attended the reception at the Russian embassy on November 7, 1946, celebrating the twenty-ninth anniversary of Russia's "Great October Socialist Revolution."

The Russian embassy was quite a place. Derevyanko arrived late in 1945 with a nominal staff of sixty. This grew to eighty-three within a month. Within a year there were 450 Russians at the embassy. This was just about four times as many American officials as occupy the United States embassy in Moscow today; it was about the same number of officials the Russians maintain within the United States today, ostensibly diplomats, most of them engaged in military and commercial espionage, in propaganda work, and in contacting members of the Communist "underground," who are kept supplied with dollars and ideas. (In contrast, too, the British started off with a staff of twenty in Tokyo and hardly ever went over thirty-five.)

MacArthur in dealing with the Russians was unlikely to forget this: in Japan, and even at the Foreign Ministers' Conference in Moscow in December 1945, the Russians ran off a film entitled *Defeat of Japan*. Naturally it showed that Russia had won the war in the Pacific single-handed. Worst of all, the end of the film showed a Russian general on the *Missouri* accepting the Japanese surrender aboard an unidentified battleship. MacArthur, Halsey, Wainwright, and the other "brass" in the background had been carefully "blacked out" by an expert Soviet film technician who must have had to do it frame by frame on the celluloid.

"Well," remarked one of the Americans who saw the newsreel in Moscow, "our hosts have done what no one else could—crowded Douglas MacArthur into the wings."

The Russian attitude was all the more galling to MacArthur because as a practitioner of democracy he had gone to the length of springing from Japan's jails the leading Communists and left-wingers who had languished there under totalitarianism for periods up to fifteen years. Much as he hated Communism, MacArthur believed in freedom of speech, provided it did not descend to license. In the fall of 1945 he turned the key in the jails that let loose the "number-two boy" in the Communist party, a smooth-talking clever fellow named Kyuichi Tokuda, later to become editor of *Akahata* ("Red Star"), the Red paper in Tokyo. Also, MacArthur permitted the top Communist of all, Sanzo

Nosaka, who had been "at school" in Yenan, China, for most of the war to re-enter Japan.

MacArthur wasted no time in lashing out at falsehoods in *Akahata*. He said the paper was ignorant of the essential of democracy when it attacked his policies on demanding that labor groups conduct themselves peacefully whenever they held public demonstrations. MacArthur again reminded the Allied Council that it was an advisory and not "an investigative or inquisitory body."

Just as Malik, Gromyko, and others have used the United Nations as a propaganda sounding board, Derevyanko tried to use the council in Japan. Frequently he asserted that MacArthur had failed to purge the Diet of so-called war criminals. Atcheson really infuriated the Russians in October 1946 by remarking off the cuff that "the time has come when Japanese aims have become virtually identical with Allied aims."

Derevyanko liked to heckle MacArthur. He would ask, for example, "How about the progress in destruction of Japanese armaments and war matériel?" MacArthur always had an answer for that one. Atcheson would reply for him: "A complete report is impossible because five letters to the Russian delegate asking for information on the disposition of Japanese troops and equipment in Russian-occupied areas have gone unanswered."

The Russians, of course, were indoctrinating their Japanese captives and sending them back to Japan piecemeal as excellent propagandists. The captured Japanese equipment is to some extent being used against us in Korea today.

In January this year the Russians walked out of the council rather than discuss the fate of the Japanese prisoners of war. The American delegate, William J. Sebald, who by then had replaced the late Mr. Atcheson, read a note that Secretary of State Dean Acheson had just handed to the Russian Ambassador in Washington.

The note asked Moscow to agree to an impartial inquiry into the fate of the prisoners of war. It recalled that Tass, the Soviet news agency, had reported in May 1949 that only 95,000 Japanese remained in Russian hands. It cited official Japanese Government figures that 376,929 Japanese soldiers were still in Russian areas. There the matter rests. It is still a useful issue to raise in Japan from time to time against the Russians.

MacArthur really blew his top against the Russians when Derevyanko, on orders from Moscow, wrote a letter charging MacArthur with sitting idly by while the Japanese Government balked democratization of the country and was crushing human rights by police brutality. This was on June 13, 1949—one Jap had been killed in small riots around Tokyo City Hall.

Departing from his usual practice of ignoring Derevyanko's letters as propaganda, MacArthur accused Russia of inciting disorder and violence in otherwise peaceful Japan. He called Derevyanko's letter "thorough duplicity" and "inconsistent demagoguery."

Derevyanko played an endless variety of critical themes against the occupation. He assailed the land reform bill. He claimed that the Americans were secretly reviving the Japanese Army by expanding the police force. He demanded that MacArthur round up and destroy all Fascist books and pamphlets in Japan.

But even Derevyanko grudgingly admitted that he had "no doubt that there is some success in the progress of the democratization of Japan."

At one point the council decided it would ask MacArthur for copies of all directives exchanged between him and the Japanese Government. MacArthur replied that the council had enough material which, if digested, would bring it fully abreast of the situation. The Russians asked for more information on the purge of militarists. MacArthur said he'd give them everything "if it takes all summer."

Between the Atcheson and Sebald tenures on the council for the Americans there were other spokesmen. One was Major General William Marquat, one-time newspaperman from Bellingham, Washington, who was MacArthur's anti-aircraft chief in the war and later chief of the economic and scientific section of Tokyo headquarters. Another was Brigadier General Courtney Whitney, former Manila lawyer and long-time friend of MacArthur, who ran the government section at headquarters.

General Whitney shot a three-hour speech at the Russians one day. Even the British and the Chinese objected, somewhat mildly. General Marquat said any time limit on presentation of material from MacArthur "would be an infringement of free speech." General Whitney added that the council members should "not pry into the Supreme Commander's armor for soft spots or seek to find material for international sensations."

"When America gives her good will and understanding," said he, "she expects a return of the same."

At another point Derevyanko, whose communications with Moscow were torpid, asked for a week's advance notice on directives that MacArthur would issue to the Japanese. MacArthur said no; any time lag would bog down the business of occupation; he would continue to give forty-eight hours' notice.

Derevyanko slammed in twenty-two recommendations on the handling of Japanese labor. MacArthur batted them all back. "We are not pledged," he said, "to further Communism in Japan."

He was solidly backed by Secretary of State Acheson.

In June of this year MacArthur rammed home one more shot: he banned the Red paper *Akahata* for thirty days for its sinister propaganda. In July he told the Japanese Government to maintain the ban indefinitely.

"In the great struggle which is now engaging the forces of the free world all segments must faithfully fulfill their share of the attendant responsibility," said MacArthur. The Reds, he said, were using media of public information to advance their tenets of subversion and violence.

He then purged from public life twenty-three members of the Communist Central Committee, including six who were members of parliament. This was aimed directly at Nosaka and Tokuda.

Nosaka, a slim, quiet character who might have been at home in a Greenwich Village "advanced" school, had spent sixteen years outside Japan. "Not for a minute," he used to mouth, "have I forgotten my land or ceased to fight for humanity. . . . Democracy is yet far away, though people yearn for it."

Nosaka remained out of jail. Sixty-three of his sympathizers were behind bars in 1948 and 1949 for criticizing unjustly the occupation of the Allies. Of Japan's 80,-000,000 people, 3,000,000 might vote Communist in an election. On signal 100,000 would "demonstrate" in Tokyo.

Last January's elections to the Diet were, in MacArthur's words, "a contest between MacArthur and Stalin." MacArthur won. He still holds "the American beachhead in Asia."

13. Hold or Die

General Douglas MacArthur kept the Russians frustrated and balked at the council table in Japan. They met him, indirectly, on a new field of conflict on June 24, 1950—in Korea. Once again MacArthur had been thrown into the breech; once again he was expected to perform miracles with very little. Was it true then, as White House insiders whispered, that General MacArthur had sent a message to President Truman which said: "You have handed me another Bataan"? If it was, nobody had confirmed it. But MacArthur must have thought along those lines as he made the dreadful decision to throw what little strength he had piecemeal into the Korean battle. Perhaps, too, MacArthur remembered his words to aging President Syngman Rhee in August of 1948, when the Republic of Korea formally came into being: "I will defend Korea as I would my own country, just as I would California."

He is now defending it; as Supreme Commander of the United Nations Forces in Korea he is leading units from nearly all the freedom-loving countries of the world. But how had it all come about? How was it that in this year of 1950, only five years after the greatest conflict in the world's history, man was again destroying man? Who was responsible for it? And was this the fore-runner of a third world war?

Korea was simply the excuse. A land which has some-times been called "The Hermit Nation," it covers a peninsula of 85,246 square miles jutting out like a tiny crooked finger between the scimitar sweep of Japan and the blunt posterior of China. It is a country of black and gray granite mountains, rice fields, heavily walled cities, pagoda temples climbing into the sky from ter-raced hillsides. Korea claims the invention of the spin-ning wheel (1376), movable type (1403), scientific instruments (1438–67), and the world's first battleship. It has a population of approximately 31,000,000 people distinct in race from the Chinese and the Japanese. They are descendants of the nomadic tribes of Mongolia and the Caucasian people of western Asia; they have both occidental and oriental characteristics, which is the reason they have often been called the "White People of the Orient."

Few people were familiar with Korea (which means "Land of the Morning Calm") until the ending of World War II.

Soviet Russia agreed to enter the Pacific war three months after the formal ending of hostilities in Europe. Thus on August 8, 1945, the Soviet Union declared war against Japan—this only a few days before the war officially ended. The United States Government sug-gested to Russia that the Red Army accept the surrender of Japanese troops north of the 38th Parallel, which cuts the country exactly in half, while American troops took the Japanese surrender in the southern half. "After this surrender had been accepted by Generalissimo Stalin," said the State Department, "it was incorporated in the first General Order which General MacArthur, as

Supreme Commander for the Allied Powers, caused to be issued on September 2, 1945. The United States did not contemplate a lasting division of Korea along this line, which was a fortuitous line resulting from the exigencies of war."

It is ironical today to learn how that line was decided upon. According to one report several one-star generals came rushing into an office in the Pentagon one day in September 1945 saying, "We have to divide Korea. Where can we divide it?" A colonel with Far East experience protested. "But we must separate the country," said the generals. The colonel exploded: "But you can't! Korea is an economic and social unit. There is no place to divide it." The generals insisted: "We have to divide Korea and it has to be done by four o'clock." So Korea was divided by four o'clock. Nobody with any political knowledge of the situation was consulted. Of course nobody asked the Koreans—it was only their country.

The Russians occupied their area (population, approximately 9,500,000) August 12, 1945; we occupied our half (population, 20,000,000) August 8, 1945. When the surrender was effected, says the State Department: "It soon became apparent that the division of Korea for surrender purposes was to be arbitrarily interpreted by the Soviet authorities as creating a permanent delineation between the two military zones, passage between which was possible only by permission of the military commanders. This situation continued despite persistent efforts of the United States Commander to negotiate arrangements with his Soviet counterpart with a view to establishing the essential unity of the country."

The Soviets, even then planning to take over China, had no intention of moving out of North Korea. They held the industrial half of the country; we the agricultural half. For two years the Russians blocked every effort to settle the question. Finally the United States put the question up to the United Nations; the Soviet countered with: "This has nothing to do with the United Nations." But the General Assembly authorized an election under the sponsorship of a United Nations commission. Again the Soviets countered: refused to let the commission operate in North Korea. The country north of the 38th Parallel was swallowed up, became part of the Iron Curtain countries. The Soviets established a "People's Democratic Republic" under the presidency of a Moscow-trained stooge, Kim Li Sung, at Pyongyang. "We are watching," said General MacArthur, "international predatory banditry in Asia."

Hundreds of Soviet agencies opened throughout North Korea; thousands of Soviet "specialists" arrived to "help" the new "People's Government." A new army was built—an army containing powerful Russian tanks and weapons—of nearly 100,000 men under Soviet-trained North Korean officers.

In the Southern Zone the Republic of Korea was accepted by the United Nations in December 1948. It was the only officially recognized government in Korea.

Dr. Syngman Rhee was named first president and said on his acceptance:

"On this day of national rejoicing our joy is clouded with sorrow as we look to the north. Nearly ten million of our fellow citizens who wished to be part of this body have been prevented from taking part in the establishment of the Republic of Korea by the refusal of the U.S.S.R. to permit the United Nations commission to observe free elections in that part of Korea occupied by the Soviets."

The South Koreans had an army of about 96,000 men

but without tanks, planes, or heavy artillery. An American military mission of a few hundred men helped them set up this army.

This, then, was the background when at 4 A.M. on June 24 heavy, well-armored North Korean columns moved south in driving rain across the 38th Parallel. The South Koreans bent before the onrush. "We were attacked by the South Koreans," yelled the North Korean propagandists. Said Moscow radio: "The U.S.S.R. has only one aim—to keep the peace."

General MacArthur promptly alerted the whole Far Eastern Command, snapped a report of the aggression to Washington, evacuated American citizens from Seoul, and rushed what military equipment he could to the embattled South Koreans. The West worked fast too. The next day President Truman ordered United States sea and air forces into action, and twenty-four hours later the United Nations Security Council backed him and called from its member nations to "furnish such assistance to the Republic of Korea as may be necessary to repel the armed attack and restore international peace and security. . . ." Truman ordered United States ground forces into action. MacArthur was given a new honor: he was named Supreme Commander for the United Nations in Korea. Some Washington wits promptly dubbed him "SCUNK."

When the war began General MacArthur had only about 400 planes at his disposal and four infantry divisions in Japan. The Navy was strongest in the Pacific area, with some twenty warships, including the aircraft carrier *Valley Forge*. He committed all the forces he could without completely denuding the Japanese islands and other strategic areas. Units of the 7th Fleet were ordered off to Formosa, which seemed to be the next

move of the Communists in Asia. These measures were
only "policing movements," warned President Truman,
but at the same time "the attack on Korea makes it
plain that Communism has passed beyond the use of
subversion to conquer independent nations and will now
use armed invasion and war."

MacArthur had long seen the United States' role in
Asia, for he had repeatedly warned: "It is here in Asia
that the first guns of the next war will sound."

At his headquarters MacArthur sent orders all over
the Pacific to his commanders. World War II bombers
from Okinawa and Iwo Jima unleashed their rusty five-
year-old bombs on North Korean bridges, marshaling
yards and munition dumps; jets slashed into motorized
convoys of troops as they cut down through South Korea.
Then, to "find out for himself," MacArthur left for the
front despite the protests of his aides and advisers. "You
can only tell how an army is fighting by being up with
the men at the front," he told them.

As his plane gradually approached the war zone a
Russian Yak fighter (the North Koreans have been flying Yaks) approached. MacArthur looked out calmly
and said to the correspondents: "We'll get him easily."
But his pilot took no chances, banked, and moved out
of the danger zone. Then MacArthur dictated battle
orders, and a few minutes later they landed. The General went straight to the front; was once again under
enemy fire. He witnessed an artillery duel, and, despite
the worries of his aides, insisted on inspecting troops and
their gun emplacements. Once, on another tour in
World War II, an aide suggested to him that he take
cover. MacArthur said: "The only reason you want me
to take cover is because you are afraid of being hit." On
this tour of the South Korean front MacArthur didn't

like what he saw. His troops were young and inexperienced, they were being outgunned by superior tanks, but they were not being outfought. They were fighting back with every weapon they possessed and with all the tenacity they could muster against a fierce, ruthless enemy.

Returning to Japan, MacArthur called Washington for men, planes, and equipment. "We are trading lives for time," he said.

As our troops gradually retreated before the fierceness of the attack Lieutenant General Walton Walker told his officers: "Hold or die—we cannot retreat any farther —there is nowhere to retreat to. There is no thought in the mind of anybody in this army—even though we might so be disposed—that there can possibly be a Dunkirk. It would be impossible to get out."

With their back to the sea in an ever-closing arc about the Port of Pusan, United States troops fought on. Heavy 3.5-inch bazookas rushed in by air began to take their toll of the enemy's tanks. But still the enemy continued to attack. General MacArthur was still confident: "I am completely confirmed in my estimates to President Truman . . . that the enemy has lost his chance for victory. This does not mean that victory passes to us instantly, or without a long, hard row and difficult struggle. That we will have new heartaches and new setbacks is inherent in the situation, but I was never more confident of victory—ultimate victory—in my life than I am now."

A few days later reinforcements began to arrive. Then the cocky, confident Marines disembarked at Pusan. "Hi, Mac, we're back!" they yelled good-naturedly as they walked down the gangplanks. Then, as they climbed on board trucks heading for the front only some thirty miles away from this last escape port, a gum-chewing Marine said to a G.I.: "What have you guys been doin' here, playin' marbles?"

Yes, the Marines were back. The G.I.s were back; so were the Air Force and the Navy fighting under a seventy-year-old soldier whose history reads like an extraordinary novel. MacArthur was once more defending "our frontiers in Asia" as he has done most of his life, as his father did before him. One thing was certain, that no matter what happened in the Pacific, General Douglas MacArthur would continue to feel just as he did ten days before the bloody holocaust of the Korean war:

"There is nothing in God's world more sure than this: Come what may, the United States is not going to scuttle in the Pacific."

General of the Army Douglas MacArthur, Supreme Commander of the Allied Powers for Japan, Supreme Commander for the United Nations in Korea, was going to make absolutely sure of that.

Appendix

MacARTHUR ON WAR

General MacArthur has never forgotten his old Rainbow Division. This speech was delivered by him at a reunion of the division in Washington prior to his retirement as Chief of Staff in 1935. Eloquently delivered, it clearly shows MacArthur's grasp of the art of war. This is perhaps his most famous speech:

Mr. President and Gentlemen of the Rainbow: I thank you for the warmth of your greeting. It moves me deeply. It was with you I lived my greatest moments. It is of you I have my greatest memories.

It was seventeen years ago—those days of old have vanished tone and tint: they have gone glimmering through the dreams of things that were. Their memory is a land where flowers of wondrous beauty and varied colors spring, watered by tears and coaxed and caressed into fuller bloom by the smiles of yesterday. Refrains no longer rise and fall from that land of used-to-be. We listen vainly but with thirsty ear for the witching melodies of days that are gone. . . . Ghosts in olive drab and sky blue and German gray pass before our eyes; voices that have stolen away in the echoes from the battlefields no more ring out. The faint far whisper of forgotten songs no longer floats through the air. Youth . . . strength . . . aspirations . . . struggles . . .

triumphs . . . despairs . . . wide winds sweeping . . .
beacons flashing across uncharted depths . . . movements . . . vividness . . . radiance . . . shadows . . .
faint bugles sounding reveille . . . far drums beating
the long roll . . . the crash of guns . . . the rattle of
musketry . . . the still white crosses . . .

And now, we are met to remember.

The shadows are lengthening. The Division's birth-
days are multiplying: we are growing old together. But
the story which we commemorate helps us grow old
gracefully. That story is known to all of you. It needs
no profuse panegyrics. It is the story of the American
soldier of the World War. My estimate of him was
formed on the battlefield many years ago and has never
changed. I regarded him then as I regard him now as
one of the world's greatest figures—not only in the era
which witnessed his achievements, but for all eyes and
for all time. I regarded him not only as one of the greatest military figures, but also as one of the most stainless;
his name and fame are the birthright of every American
citizen.

The world's estimate of him will be founded not upon
any one battle or even series of battles: indeed, it is not
upon the greatest fields of combat or the bloodiest that
the recollections of future ages are riveted. The vast
theaters of Asiatic conflict are already forgotten today.
The slaughtered myriads of Genghis Khan lie in undis-
tinguished graves. Hardly a pilgrim visits the scenes
where on the fields of Châlons and Tours the destinies
of civilization and Christendom were fixed by the skill
of Aetius and the valor of Charles Martel.

The time indeed may come when the memory of the
fields of Champagne and Picardy, of Verdun and the
Argonne shall be dimmed by the obscurity of revolving

years and recollected only as a shadow of ancient days.

But even then the enduring fortitude, the patriotic self-abnegation, and the unsurpassed military genius of the American soldier needs no eulogy from me or from any other man; he has written his own history, and it is written in red on his enemy's breast but when I think of his patience under adversity, of his courage under fire, and of his modesty in victory, I am filled with an emotion I cannot express. He belongs to history as furnishing one of the greatest examples of successful and disinterested patriotism. He belongs to posterity as the instructor of future generations in the principles of liberty and right. He belongs to the present—to us—by his glory, by his virtues, and by his achievements.

The memorials of character wrought by him can never be dimmed. He needs no statues or monuments; he has stamped himself in blazing flames upon the souls of his countrymen; he has carved his own statue in the hearts of his people; he has built his own monument in the memory of his compatriots.

The military code which he perpetuates has come down to us from even before the age of knighthood and chivalry. It embraces the highest moral laws, and will stand the text of any ethics or philosophies ever promulgated for the uplift of mankind. Its requirements are for the things that are right, and its restraints are from the things that are wrong. Its observance will uplift everyone who comes under its influence. The soldier, above all other men, is required to perform the highest act of religious teaching . . . sacrifice. In battle and in the face of danger and death he discloses those divine attributes which his Maker gave him when He created man in His own image. No physical courage and no brute instincts can take the place of the divine annunciation and spiritual uplift which will alone sustain him. However horrible the incidents of war may be, the soldier who is called upon to offer and to give his life for his country is the noblest development of mankind.

On such an occasion as this my thoughts go back to those men who went with us to their last charge. In memory's eye I can see them now—forming grimly for the attack, blue-lipped, covered with sludge and mud, chilled by the wind and rain of the fox-hole, driving home to their objective, and to the Judgment Seat of God. I do not know the dignity of their birth, but I do know the glory of their death. They died unquestioning, uncomplaining, with faith in their hearts, and on their lips the hope that we would go on to victory.

Never again for them staggering columns, bending under soggy packs on many a weary march from dripping dusk to drizzling dawn. Never again will they slug ankle deep through the mud on shell-shocked roads. Never again will they stop cursing their luck long enough to whistle through chapped lips a few bars as some clear voice raised the lilt of "Madelon." Never again ghastly trenches with their maze of tunnels, drifts, pits, dugouts —never again. Gentlemen unafraid.

They have gone beyond the mists that blind us here, and become part of that beautiful thing we call the spirit of the unknown soldier. In chambered temples of silence the dust of their dauntless valor sleeps, waiting, waiting in the Chancery of Heaven the final reckoning of Judgment Day. "Only those are fit to live who are not afraid to die."

Our country is rich and resourceful, populous and progressive—courageous to the full extent of propriety. It insists upon respect for its rights, and likewise gives full recognition to the rights of all others. It stands for peace, honesty, fairness, and friendship in its intercourse with foreign nations. . . . It has become a strong, influential, and leading factor in world affairs. It is destined to be even greater if our people are sufficiently wise to improve their manifold opportunities. If we are industrious, economical, and absolutely fair in our treatment of each other, strictly loyal to our government, we, the people, may expect to be prosperous and to remain secure in the enjoyment of all those benefits which this privileged land affords.

But, so long as humanity is more or less governed by motives not in accord with the spirit of Christianity, our country may be involved by those who believe they are more powerful, whatever the ostensible reason advanced may be—envy, cupidity, fancied wrong, or other unworthy impulse may direct.

Every nation that has what is valuable is obligated to be prepared to defend against brutal attack or unjust effort to seize and appropriate. Even though a man be not inclined to guard his own interests, common decency requires him to furnish reasonable oversight and care to others who are weak and helpless. As a rule they who preach by word or by deed, "Peace at any price," are not possessed of anything worth having, and are oblivious to the interests of others, including their own dependents.

The Lord Almighty, merciful and all wise, does not absolutely protect those who unreasonably fail to contribute to their own safety, but He does help those who, to the limit of their understanding and ability, help themselves. This, my friends, is fundamental theology.

On looking back through the history of English-speaking people, it will be found in every instance that the most sacred principles of free government have been acquired, protected, and perpetuated through the embodied, armed strength of the peoples concerned. From Magna Charta to the present day there is little in our institutions worth having or worth perpetuating that has not been achieved for us by armed men. Trade, wealth, literature, and refinement cannot defend a state—pacific habits do not insure peace or immunity from national insult and national aggression.

Every nation that would preserve its tranquillity, its riches, its independence, and its self-respect, must keep alive its martial ardor and be at all times prepared to defend itself!

The United States is a pre-eminently Christian and conservative nation. It is far less militaristic than most nations. It is not especially open to the charge of imperialism. Yet, one would fancy that Americans were the most brutally bloodthirsty people in the world, to judge by the frantic efforts that are being made to disarm them both physically and morally. The public opinion of the United States is being submerged by a deluge of organizations whose activities to prevent war would be understandable were they distributed in some degree among the armed nations of Europe and Asia. The effect of all of this unabashed and unsound propaganda is not so much to convert America to a holy horror of war as it is to confuse the public mind and lead to muddled thinking in international affairs.

A few intelligent groups who are vainly trying to present the true facts to the world are overwhelmed by the sentimentalist, the emotionalist, the alarmist, who merely befog the real issue which is not the biological necessity of war but the biological character of war.

The springs of human conflict cannot be eradicated

through institutions but only through the reform of the individual human being. And *that* is a task which has baffled the highest theologians for two thousand years and more.

I often wonder how the future historian in the calmness of his study will analyze the civilization of the century recently closed. It was ushered in by the end of the Napoleonic Wars which devastated half of Europe. Then followed the Mexican War, the American Civil War, the Crimean War, the Austro-Prussian War, the Franco-Prussian War, the Boer War, the opium wars of England and China, the Spanish-American War, the Russo-Japanese War and, finally, the World War— which, for ferocity and magnitude of losses, is unequaled in the history of humanity.

If he compares this record of human slaughter with the thirteenth century, when civilization was just emerging from the Dark Ages, when literature had its Dante; art its Michelangelo and Gothic architecture; education, the establishment of the famous colleges and technical schools of Europe; medicine, the organization of the hospital system; and politics, the foundation of Anglo-Saxon liberty, the Magna Charta—the verdict cannot be that wars have been on the wane.

In the last thirty-four hundred years only two hundred and sixty-eight—less than one in thirteen—have been free from wars. No wonder that Plato, that wisest of all men, once exclaimed, "Only the dead have seen the end of war!" Every reasonable man knows that war is cruel and destructive. Yet, our civilization is such that a very little of the fever of war is sufficient to melt its veneer of kindliness. We all dream of the day when human conduct will be governed by the Decalogue and the Sermon on the Mount. But as yet it is only a dream. No one desires peace as much as the soldier, for he must pay the greatest penalty in war. Our army is maintained solely for the preservation of peace—or, for the restoration of peace after it has been lost by statesmen or by others.

Dionysius, the ancient thinker, twenty centuries ago uttered these words: "It is a law of nature, common to all mankind which time shall neither annul nor destroy, that those that have greater strength and power shall bear rule over those who have less." Unpleasant as they may be to hear, disagreeable as they may be to contemplate, the history of the world bears ample testimony to their truth and wisdom. When looking over the past, or when looking over the world in its present form, there is but one trend of events to be discerned—a constant change of tribes, clans, nations, the stronger ones replacing the others, the more vigorous ones pushing aside, absorbing, covering with oblivion the weak and the worn out.

From the dawn of history to the present day it has always been the militant aggressor taking the place of the unprepared. Where are the empires of old? Where is Egypt, once a state on a high plane of civilization where a form of socialism prevailed and where the distribution of wealth *was* regulated? Her high organization did not protect her. Where are the empires of the East and the empires of the West which once were the shrines of wealth, wisdom, and culture? Where are Babylon, Persia, Carthage, Rome, Byzantium? They all fell, never to rise again—annihilated at the hands of a more warlike and aggressive people. Their cultures, memories—their cities, ruins.

Where are Peru and old Mexico? A handful of bold

and crafty invaders destroyed them—and with them their institutions, their independence, their nationality, and their civilization.

And saddest of all the downfall of Christian Byzantium. When Constantinople fell, that center of learning, pleasure, and wealth—and all the weakness and corruption that goes with it—a pall fell over Asia and southeastern Europe which has never been lifted. Wars have been fought these nearly five centuries that have had for at least one of their goals the bringing back under the Cross of that part of the world lost to a wild horde of a few thousand adventurers on horseback whom hunger and the unkind climate of their steppes forced to seek more fertile regions.

The thousand years of existence of the Byzantine Empire, its size, its religion, the wealth of its capital city were but added incentives and inducements to an impecunious conqueror. For wealth is no protection against aggression. It is no more an augury of military and defensive strength in a nation than it is an indication of health in an individual. Success in war depends upon men, not money. No nation has ever been subdued for lack of it. Indeed, nothing is more insolent or provocative or more apt to lead to a breach of the peace than undefended riches among armed men.

And each nation swept away was submerged by force of arms. Once each was strong and militant, each rose by military prowess, each fell through degeneracy of military capacity because of unpreparedness. The battlefield was the bed upon which they were born into this world and the battlefield became the couch on which their worn-out bodies finally expired. Let us be prepared, lest we, too, perish.

They will tell of the peace eternal
    And we would wish them well.
They will scorn the path of war's red wrath
    And brand it the road to hell.
They will set aside their warrior pride
    And their love for the soldier sons.
But at last they will turn again
    To horse, and foot, and guns.

They will tell of the peace eternal.
    The Assyrian dreamers did.
But the Tigris and the Euphrates ran
      through ruined lands.
    And amid the hopeless chaos
Loud they wept and called their chosen ones
    To save their lives at the bitter last,
With horse, and foot, and guns.

They will tell of the peace eternal,
    And may that peace succeed.
But what of a foe that lurks to spring?
    And what of a nation's need?
The letters blaze on history's page,
    And ever the writing runs,
God, and honor, and native land,
    And horse, and foot, and guns.

MacARTHUR ON GENGHIS KHAN

The following is an excerpt from General MacArthur's report of 1935 to the Secretary of War when he was Chief of Staff:

More than most professions the military is forced to depend upon intelligent interpretation of the past for signposts charting the future. Devoid of opportunity, in peace, for self-instruction through actual practice of his profession, the soldier makes maximum use of historical record in assuring the readiness of himself and his command to function efficiently in emergency. The facts derived from historical analysis he applies to conditions of the present and the proximate future, thus developing a synthesis of appropriate method, organization, and doctrine.

But the military student does not seek to learn from history the minutiae of method and technique. In every age these are decisively influenced by the characteristics of weapons currently available and by the means at hand for maneuvering, supplying, and controlling combat forces. But research does bring to light those fundamental principles, and their combinations and applications, which, in the past, have been productive of success. These principles know no limitation of time. Consequently, the army extends its analytical interest to the dust-buried accounts of wars long past as well as to those still reeking with the scent of battle. It is the object of the search that dictates the field for its pursuit. Those callow critics who hold that only in the most recent battles are there to be found truths applicable to our present problems have failed utterly to see this. They apparently cling to a fatuous hope that in historical study is to be found a complete digest of the science of war rather than simply the basic and inviolable laws of the art of war.

Were the accounts of all battles, save only those of Genghis Khan, effaced from the pages of history, and were the facts of his campaigns preserved in descriptive detail, the soldier would still possess a mine of untold wealth from which to extract nuggets of knowledge useful in molding an army for future use. The successes of that amazing leader, beside which the triumphs of most other commanders in history pale into insignificance, are proof sufficient of his unerring instinct for the fundamental qualifications of an army.

He devised an organization appropriate to conditions then existing; he raised the discipline and the morale of his troops to a level never known in any other army, unless possibly that of Cromwell; he spent every available period of peace to develop subordinate leaders and to produce perfection of training throughout the army, and, finally, he insisted upon speed in action, a speed which by comparison with other forces of his day was almost unbelievable. Though he armed his men with the best equipment of offense and of defense that the skill of Asia could produce, he refused to encumber them with loads that would immobilize his army. Over great distances his legions moved so rapidly and secretly as to astound his enemies and practically to paralyze their powers of resistance. He crossed great rivers and mountain ranges, he reduced walled cities in his path and swept onward to destroy nations and pulverize whole civilizations. On the battlefield his troops maneuvered so swiftly and skillfully and struck with such devastating speed that times without number they defeated armies overwhelmingly superior to themselves in numbers.

Regardless of his destructiveness, his cruelty, his savagery, he clearly understood the unvarying necessities of war. It is these conceptions that the modern soldier seeks to separate from the details of the Khan's technique, tactics, and organization, as well as from the ghastly practices of his butcheries, his barbarism, and his ruthlessness. So winnowed from the chaff of medieval custom and of all other inconsequentials, they stand revealed as kernels of eternal truth, as applicable today in our effort to produce an efficient army as they were when, seven centuries ago, the great Mongol applied them to the discomfiture and amazement of a terrified world. We cannot violate these laws and still produce and sustain the kind of army that alone can insure the integrity of our country and the permanency of our institutions if ever again we face the grim realities of war.

MacARTHUR ON PEACE

MacArthur's hands shook a little as the surrender papers were signed on board the battleship *Missouri* in Tokyo Bay on September 2, 1945. The Pacific war was ended. For MacArthur it had been a long, bitter struggle. His voice trembling with emotion, he made this concluding speech:

My fellow countrymen:

Today the guns are silent. A great tragedy has ended. A great victory has been won. The skies no longer rain death—the seas bear only commerce—men everywhere walk upright in the sunlight. The entire world is quietly at peace. The holy mission has been completed, and in reporting this to you, the people, I speak for the thousands of silent lips, forever stilled, among the jungles and the beaches and in the deep waters of the Pacific which marked the way. I speak for the unnamed brave millions homeward bound to take up the challenge of that future which they did so much to salvage from the brink of disaster.

As I look back on the long, tortuous trail from those grim days of Bataan and Corregidor, when an entire world lived in fear; when democracy was on the defensive everywhere, when modern civilization trembled in the balance, I thank a merciful God that He has given us the faith, the courage, and the power from which to mold victory.

We have known the bitterness of defeat and the exultation of triumph, and from both we have learned there can be no turning back. We must go forward to preserve in peace what we won in war.

A new era is upon us. Even the lesson of victory itself brings with it profound concern, both for our future security and the survival of civilization. The destructiveness of the war potential, through progressive advances in scientific discovery, has in fact now reached a point which revised the traditional concept of war.

Men since the beginning of time have sought peace. Various methods through the ages have attempted to devise an international process to prevent or settle disputes between nations. From the very start workable methods were found in so far as individual citizens were concerned, but the mechanics of an instrumentality of larger international scope have never been successful. Military alliance, balances of power, league of nations all in turn failed, leaving the only path to be by way of the crucible of war.

The utter destructiveness of war now blots out this alternative. We have had our last chance. If we do not now devise some greater and more equitable system Armageddon will be at our door. The problem basically is theological and involves a spiritual recrudescence and improvement of human character that will synchronize with our almost matchless advance in science, art, literature, and all material and cultural developments of the past two thousand years. It must be of the spirit if we are to save the flesh.

We stand in Tokyo today reminiscent of our countryman, Commodore Perry, ninety-two years ago. His purpose was to bring to Japan an era of enlightenment and progress by lifting the veil of isolation to the friendship, trade, and commerce of the world. But alas the knowledge thereby gained of Western science was forged into an instrument of oppression and human enslavement. Freedom of expression, freedom of action, even freedom of thought were denied through suppression of liberal education, through appeal to superstition and through the application of force.

We are committed by the Potsdam Declaration of principles to see that the Japanese people are liberated from this condition of slavery. It is my purpose to implement this commitment just as rapidly as the armed forces are demobilized and other essential steps taken to neutralize the war potential. The energy of the Japanese race, if properly directed, will enable expansion vertically rather than horizontally. If the talents of the race are turned into constructive channels, the country can lift itself from its present deplorable state into a position of dignity.

To the Pacific basin has come the vista of a new emancipated world. Today, freedom is on the offensive, democracy is on the march. Today, in Asia as well as in Europe, unshackled peoples are tasting the full sweetness of liberty, the relief from fear.

In the Philippines, America has evolved a model for this new free world of Asia. In the Philippines, America has demonstrated that peoples of the East and peoples of the West may walk side by side in mutual respect and with mutual benefit. The history of our sovereignty there has now the full confidence of the East.

And so, my fellow countrymen, today I report to you that your sons and daughters have served you well and faithfully with the calm, deliberate, determined fighting spirit of the American soldier and sailor based upon a tradition of historical trait, as against the fanaticism of any enemy supported only by mythological fiction, their spiritual strength and power have brought us through to victory. They are homeward bound—take care of them.